Managing Social Responsibility in Universities

Loreta Tauginienė · Raminta Pučėtaitė
Editors

Managing Social Responsibility in Universities

Organisational Responses to Sustainability

Editors
Loreta Tauginienė
Hanken School of Economics
Helsinki, Finland

Raminta Pučėtaitė
Kaunas Faculty
Vilnius University
Vilnius, Lithuania

ISBN 978-3-030-70012-6   ISBN 978-3-030-70013-3   (eBook)
https://doi.org/10.1007/978-3-030-70013-3

Cover illustration: © John Rawsterne/patternhead.com

This Palgrave Macmillan imprint is published by the registered company Springer Nature Switzerland AG
The registered company address is: Gewerbestrasse 11, 6330 Cham, Switzerland

FOREWORD

We live in a world in which many institutions are called upon to be 'socially responsible'. These institutions include not only big corporations but also small- and medium-sized companies, entrepreneurial firms, as well as civil society organizations and non-governmental organizations. So, why would social responsibility not be a relevant concept for universities, too? Why should universities not also be 'socially responsible'?

I must confess that the idea of 'university social responsibility' initially struck me as somewhat problematic. Isn't it the case that universities already have a major social responsibility through their traditional mandate to advance societies, through both delivering excellent higher education for the ambitious youth and advancing scientific knowledge through facilitating research of the highest standards? Isn't exactly this the utmost 'social responsibility' of universities, their bread and butter, their *raison d'être*, so to speak? It would seem that delivering on this dual task is already a major accomplishment in these days when the educational and research budgets of universities continue to be cut back in many countries around the world. What else might be expected from them?

There is, of course, the third task of serving societies' needs. Universities are supposed to make sure that the courses and programs they offer meet the employment needs of the society in which they operate and that the research conducted under their umbrellas has societal value added. But then, upon further reflection and if we take a closer look at the employment needs, for example, it will become clear that the employment needs have become the employment needs of 'the market' and of private enterprise. Over the past decades and following this trend, there has been a shift to favor educational programs in the natural and technical sciences, medicine, economics, management, and law, at the expense of the humanities and social sciences. No longer *Bildung*, but instead the production of human intellectual capital as an instrumental and economically valuable resource for the market.

A similar shift can be observed in academic research from what was understood as addressing societal needs in the early 1970s to today's understanding (which actually has a legacy that goes back to the early 1980s). In my home country, The Netherlands, the early 1970s saw the introduction of so-called science shops, which served as entry points to academic research for disadvantaged groups and individuals who depended on scientific advice and research to help resolve the issues they were struggling with. These science shops have disappeared. And how about the debates about 'post-normal science', 'mode 2 research', 'action research', 'citizen science', and other ways of doing research that have sought to square academic research with addressing the specific societal needs, problems, and concerns that were not or could not be addressed through 'normal' fundamental or applied research; have they disappeared, too?

These days, it seems that the calls for addressing societal needs through research have become more narrowly defined as pushes for economically defined 'valorization'. For example, 'transfer offices' have been created to help researchers commercialize their findings, and public (national programs, the EU frameworks) and private research funds are increasingly demanding that bids for research funds are very explicit in how the proposed research will contribute to helping resolve relatively narrowly defined yet undoubtedly highly important issues, as identified by them. Cecil Wright Mills complained already in the late 1950s, in his *Sociological Imagination*, that much of social science research was done by researchers who effectively positioned themselves as the loyal servants of the interests of the State and corporate bureaucracies. His complaint is as relevant today as it was more than half a century ago.

This instrumentalization and economization of higher education and academic research are to be regretted and criticized as myopic and narrowminded, as has been argued in many articles and books. One such book stands out. Rens Bod's *A New History of the Humanities* (2013) is not only a history of 'the forgotten sciences'—as was the title of the original

Dutch language edition—but also a strong reminder of the many contributions that the humanities, writ large, throughout the ages and from all around the world, have made to culture and human well-being.

On the other hand, some allegedly positive developments may be pointed out when it comes to university social responsibility. Many business schools and faculties of business administration, for example, have endorsed the UN Principles for Responsible Management Education (PRME). However, these principles are tailored to specialized areas of academic activity, whereas the *university* is so much larger and encompasses so many more fields and disciplines.

So, perhaps the time is now, and maybe there is a need to re-open this debate about what are and should be the roles and functions of universities in contemporary societies. Might it be the case—in reminiscence of Richard Rorty—that we can open new avenues and perspectives in this debate if we change the language in the discourse? Can we revive and reinvigorate the old debates by relabeling them as a question of 'university social responsibility'? I hope so. May this volume be a seed for the renewal of this old debate. It is much needed.

September 2020

Frank den Hond
Ehrnrooth Professor of Management
and Organisation, Hanken School of
Economics, Helsinki, Finland

Acknowledgments

For feedback
The authors of Chapter 3 thank Frank den Hond, Ehrnrooth Professor in Management and Organisation at Hanken School of Economics (Finland) for his helpful comments on an early chapter draft as well as participants of the EAIR 41st Annual Forum 'Responsibility of Higher Education Systems: What? Why? How?', Leiden, the Netherlands, 2019 where portion of this chapter was presented.

For support
The authors of Chapter 3 are grateful to Kaunas Faculty of Vilnius University (Lithuania) for continual support to this research.

The research of the authors of Chapter 7 was supported by the Erasmus+ Programme, Strategic Partnerships under Grant number 2018-1-RO01-KA203-049309.

Contents

NOTES ON CONTRIBUTORS

Dr. Montserrat Alom Bartrolí is the Director of the International Centre for Research and Decision Support of the International Federation of Catholic Universities, Paris, France, and an Associate Researcher at CEPED-Université Paris Descartes. As a sociologist of science, she works on scientific collaborations involving the South and research funding policies.

Sara Bice is an Associate Professor and Foundation Director of the Institute for Infrastructure in Society at the Crawford School of Public Policy, The Australian National University. She is Vice Chancellor's Futures Scheme Senior Fellow for her work on The Next Generation Engagement program, Australia's largest study into community engagement in infrastructure. She is Past President, International Association for Impact Assessment, the world's leading organization for impact assessment practitioners, researchers, and clients, representing almost 7000 members in 120 different countries. Sara is an Associate Professor (Special International Guest) at the School of Public Policy and Management, Tsinghua University, Beijing.

Hamish Coates is a Tenured Professor at Tsinghua University's Institute of Education, Director of the Higher Education Research Division, and Deputy Director of the Tsinghua University Global Research Centre for the Assessment of College and Student Development. He was Professor of Higher Education at the University of Melbourne, Founding Director of Higher Education Research at the Australian Council for Educational Research, and Program Director at the LH Martin Institute for Tertiary Leadership and Management. He concentrates on improving the quality and productivity of higher education.

Dr. Gabriel Dima is Professor at the University Politehnica of Bucharest, Department of Electronics, Telecommunications & IT. Gabriel holds a Ph.D. in Microelectronics having as research interest topics like observation of education systems, policies and innovation, university social responsibility, ICT for development issues, sustainable development and responsible and inclusive research and innovation. He is a member of the General Meeting of European Association of Service Learning in Higher Education (EASLHE) and coordinates the ENGAGE STUDENTS project.

Bror Giesenbauer is researching on the topics of sustainable development, diversity management and systemic change at the University of Bremen. As a member of the project HOCH-N, he is building and managing a network for sustainability in higher education institutions. His works are focused on finding ways to enable systems—from businesses to universities—to handle increasingly complex challenges and to deal with urgent issues such as sustainable development.

Xi Hong is a Ph.D. Student at the Tsinghua University Institute of Education. Xi is the recipient of the 'Future Scholar Scholarship of Tsinghua University'. She specializes in the field of higher education, focusing in particular on student development, higher education policy, higher education assessment, and minorities.

Dr. Kenneth Mølbjerg Jørgensen is a Professor of organization studies at the Department of Urban Studies at Malmö University in Sweden. His research interests comprise power, storytelling, ethics, and sustainability in organizations. He is involved in projects concerning sustainability, technology, and inclusion. He is the director of the Gaia Storytelling Lab. Kenneth has authored, co-authored, and edited numerous books, articles, and book chapters in among others Organization, *Scandinavian Journal of Management, Business Ethics—A European Perspective*, CBS Press, Sage, and Nova.

Dr. Lu Liu is an Assistant Professor at School of Education, Jiangsu University. He graduated with bachelor's degree from Victoria University of Wellington in 2013 and master's degree from Massey University in 2015 and received his Ph.D. from Nanjing Agricultural University in 2018. From 2018 to 2020, he served as a Postdoctoral Research Fellow at Tsinghua University's Institute of Education. His research focuses on higher education policy and management between Chinese and foreign countries.

Prof. Dr. rer. pol. Georg Müller-Christ holds the Chair of Sustainable Management at the University of Bremen, Department of Economics. From 2008 until 2011, he served the University of Bremen as a Vice-rector for study affairs. Since 2009 he is the speaker of the working group for Sustainability in Higher Education Institutions, a working group of the Round Table of the UN-Decade for Education for Sustainable Development. Since 2014 Georg Müller-Christ is introducing the method of systemic constellations into science. In his scientific works, he pursues the question whether the requirements of a sustainable development can be connected to entrepreneurial decision routines.

Dr. Raminta Pučėtaitė is an Associate Professor and Senior Researcher of Business Ethics and Corporate Social Responsibility at Kaunas Faculty, Vilnius University, Lithuania and Adjunct Professor of Management, Organizational Ethics and Human Resource Management at the University of Jyväskylä School of Business and Economics, Finland. Her research encompasses values management, research and academic ethics, ethical aspects of human resource management, social entrepreneurship, and organizational innovativeness with a focus on socio-cultural context. Her research findings have been published in the *Journal of Business Ethics*, *Business Ethics: A European Review*, *Baltic Journal of Management*, *Journal of Social Entrepreneurship*, *Journal of Baltic Studies*, etc.

Dr. Katharina Resch is Postdoctoral Researcher at the University of Vienna, Center for Teacher Education and Faculty of Educational Science. Katharina holds a Ph.D. in Sociology and focuses primarily in her research on higher education research, in particular diversity, social inequality, and Service Learning. She has carried out several European Service-Learning projects (ENGAGE STUDENTS, European Student Engagement Project, UNIBILITY—University Meets Social Responsibility).

Dr. Loreta Tauginienė is an Academic Professional, lately Associated Researcher at Hanken School of Economics, Finland and formerly Researcher at Vilnius University, Faculty of Kaunas, Institute for Social Sciences and Applied Informatics. She is a part of the editorial board of *Journal of Academic Ethics* and *Journal of Management and Change*. She has published over 20 publications related to social responsibility, stakeholder engagement, science in society and integrity. Her research interests are academic/research integrity, social responsibility of higher education institutions, public engagement, citizen science and responsible research and innovation.

Dr. Merle K. Tegeler conducts research on sustainable development in teaching as well as on organizational changes at the University of Bremen. She is a member of the project HOCH-N, pursuing the idea of aligning academic teaching both didactically and thematically to sustainable development. The goal is to capture the high complexity within the system and to make it manageable for all.

LIST OF FIGURES

LIST OF TABLES

CHAPTER 1

Revisiting University Social Responsibility

Loreta Tauginienė and Raminta Pučėtaitė

Corporate social responsibility (CSR) as an organisation's collective responsibility for its impact on society has become an established concept in management scholarship since the 1990s. De Bakker, Groenewegen, and den Hond (2005) showcase the variety of institutional responsibility-related concepts since 1950, ranging from 1950 to 2002 until they were merged into CSR by Archie Carroll (1991). Since the beginning of the 1990s, CSR has received immense attention from academia, evidenced by a rise in the number of publications in the leading management journals (De Bakker et al., 2005). Nowadays, the concept has departed from an initial definition of an organisation's economic, legal, ethical, and philanthropic responsibilities as proposed by Carroll. Moreover, it is no longer considered a voluntary activity, which was a prevalent characteristic in the first decade of the 2000s (Crane, Matten, & Spence, 2008). Rather, the conceptual dimensions of economic, environmental,

L. Tauginienė (✉)
Hanken School of Economics, Helsinki, Finland
e-mail: loreta.tauginiene@hanken.fi

R. Pučėtaitė
Vilnius University, Vilnius, Lithuania
e-mail: raminta.pucetaite@knf.vu.lt

L. Tauginienė and R. Pučėtaitė (eds.), *Managing Social Responsibility in Universities*, https://doi.org/10.1007/978-3-030-70013-3_1

1

and socio-ethical responsibilities are complemented by the inclusion of diverse stakeholders in an organisation's activities, minimising its externalities, production of innovative products and services, and creating multiple values by organisational performance (European Commission, 2011; Jonker, 2012). Although the social responsibility of business has been in researchers' intense focus since then, the social responsibility of public sector organisations remains scarcely and passingly researched. Most attempts have been directed at shedding light on country-specific public sector organisations and their responsibilities to society (e.g. about India in Sangle, 2010; about Lithuania in Štreimikienė & Pušinaitė, 2009; Pauzuoliene & Mauriciene, 2013; about Poland in Hawrysz & Foltys, 2016). There are even more studies that explore roles of public sector organisations in promoting corporate social responsibility (e.g. Albareda, Lozano, Tencati, Perrini, & Midttun, 2009; Fox, Ward, & Howard, 2002; Ward, 2004). Lack of focus on public organisations' social responsibility can be explained by the very purpose of these institutions, i.e. the social responsibility of public sector organisations is considered embedded in them through their mission to serve societal interest. Hence, the congruence between the normative and the empirical of social responsibility is assumed. However, corruption scandals and ineffective use of resources in public sector have called for CSR reforms worldwide, which implies that the empirical of social responsibility does not always align with its normative implications and societal expectations. The divergence between the dimensions of normative and empirical calls for investigations on frameworks and instruments that enable their connection.

The university as a predominantly public institution with a social mission and potential for social impact is a niche for deeper investigations of its social responsibility, both conceptually and empirically. Fast changing society and technological advance demand from the university revision of teaching content and methods and also impel shifts in measurement. In some realms of university activities, like business and management education, we witness the rise of soft regulations, such as the United Nations Principles for Responsible Management Education, adopted by business schools for stronger social impact on building sustainable society globally. Another perspective on university social responsibility is offered by the concept of responsible research and innovation, promoted by the European Commission through its funding under Framework Programme 7 and Horizon2020, and by associations such as All European Academies, through its European Code of Conduct for

Research Integrity. Briefly, these notions emerged in academic debate, e.g. what is socially responsible science? (e.g. Bird, 2014). These are just a few examples of what transformations occurred (and continue to occur) when striving to proclaim social responsibility. In advanced societies, universities are large organisations themselves, facing responsibilities as an employer, a procurer, and a consumer of goods and services that can have an impact on environmental awareness through a learning setting.

Our book responds to these challenges by offering insights into evaluating and monitoring university social responsibility. We discuss the dimensions constituting university social responsibility, teaching approaches and methods that help to educate service-oriented graduates whose professionalism is manifested through accountability and responsibility to society and the Earth, and managerial practices which can help universities to become sustainable organisations. More specifically, the book opens with a study that describes how co-creation and actor-network theory contribute to the development of an assessment system of university social responsibility (Chapter 2). Montserrat Alom Bartroli describes how an artificial intelligence-based framework for Catholic higher education institutions was developed. She thoroughly explains difficulties in accommodating different understandings of university social responsibility, developing an assessment of university social responsibility, and then making preparatory steps for its launch. It is notable that co-creation was harnessed in a co-construction phase of an assessment system on university social responsibility.

Furthermore, Loreta Tauginienė and Raminta Pučėtaitė present the findings of their conceptual development of an integrative framework for measuring (and monitoring) university social responsibility from the perspective of organisational, social, environmental, and educational dimensions (Chapter 3). They conceptually capture the status and progress on 16 qualitative indicators which address short-term outcomes: it is noteworthy that no indicator remained in such dimensions as the ethical and economic. This is an interesting result considering the discourses in responsible research and good governance stemming from the United Nations Sustainable Development Goals, the European Commission's political and national legislative initiatives to ensure, e.g. gender balance in science (Marchetti & Raudma, 2010), and research funding programmes promoting gender equality in academic institutions.

The re-framing of social engagement contributions in higher education institutions is discussed by Xi Hong, Lu Liu, and Hamish Coates

(Chapter 4). Authors draw our attention to sustainability and social impact indicators as a mirror of university education; research, social and institutional growth dimensions that need new perspectives in defining education value. They mainly focus on identifying social contribution indicators and related items which emphasise openness through dynamic involvement, intersectoral and intergenerational collaboration, and so forth.

Bror Giesenbauer, Merle K. Tegeler and Georg Müller-Christ share the experience of the University of Bremen in Germany, moving from eco-centricity to sustainability in management (Chapter 5). From the transformation perspective, this case captures a historical shift of sustainability concept development and a system of values embedded in university management. In practice, it translates to moving from the environmental responsibility of an organisation, as reflected in reports on environmental performance under eco-standards, to wider ones, embracing equal opportunity, promoting sustainability in all types of study programmes through an online course on the topic, extending networking activities to enrich students' experience and deepen their awareness on the global effects their decisions and actions may have. This shift is analysed through the lens of university development stages by Clare W. Graves, postulating the rise of University 4.0 in contemporary society. At a more general level, the case illustrates how a university can respond to the contemporary challenges of internationalisation, massification, marketisation and digitisation and assume the responsibility for future generations through continual improvement.

Kenneth Mølbjerg Jørgensen calls for invoking seven storytelling principles for terrestrial management education through the lens of Hannah Arendt's notion of storytelling, leading to the "Gaia principle" or the eternal recurrence of nature's life cycles (Chapter 6). The seven principles include self-formation, problem-oriented learning, multispecies storytelling, gaiagraphy, governance, truth-telling and reflexivity, constituting a framework of the Gaia storytelling organisation. Such an organisation is noted for the awareness of place which plays a central role in terrestrial-oriented storytelling. This is a promising futuristic approach in teaching sustainability, and its practice is emerging. The author evidences the latter with a recent unique practice in Malmö University, Sweden where a new study programme has been launched. This programme combines interdisciplinarity with intersectoral focus to address sustainability in a more efficient way.

Katharina Resch and Gabriel Dima are even more specific in arguing the need for Service Learning in university education as a novel and effective teaching approach that bridges theory and practice and promotes the social responsibility of students (Chapter 7). They discuss the empirical findings from qualitative interviews with teachers from five European countries on inputs, processes of approaching community partners, and perceived outputs of Service Learning. The findings show that in many cases the adoption of the method is hindered by lack of institutional support, although there are instances of institutional inputs in the form of matching platforms and support in contractual issues. From the teachers' perspective, finding community partners is a complex process, requiring personal devotion, student involvement, and their appropriate counselling to produce results which benefit the partners and build trust. If properly applied, Service Learning may significantly contribute to students' civic engagement, work-related skills, and personal growth. The authors call for reflection on applying the approach to e-learning and what inputs it would require connecting to geographically distant communities for collaboration and to produce outcomes that align professional goals with empathetic, responsible, and systematic action.

Rather than to attempt an exhaustive study of the social responsibility of higher education institutions, our purpose in this book is to induce a more nuanced discussion on the topic. Therefore, we invite the large and increasing community of social responsibility researchers in different socio-cultural contexts to test the discussed frameworks. We hope that the different practices and points of view in the book will inspire others to continue a multi-voice discussion on the multiplicity of levels and aspects of the phenomenon and concept.

REFERENCES

Albareda, L., Lozano, J. M., Tencati, A., Perrini, F., & Midttun, A. (2009). The role of government in corporate social responsibility*. In L. Zsolnai, Z. Boda, & L. Fekete (Eds.), *Ethical prospects* (pp. 103–149). Dordrecht: Springer.

Bird, S. J. (2014). Socially responsible science is more than "good science". *Journal of Microbiology & Biology Education, 15*(2), 169–172.

Carroll, A. (1991). The pyramid of corporate social responsibility: Toward the moral management of organizational stakeholders. *Business Horizons, 34*(4), 39–48.

Crane, A., Matten, D., & Spence, L. J. (2008). *Corporate social responsibility: Readings and cases in a global context*. New York: Routledge.

De Bakker, F. G. A., Groenewegen, P., & den Hond, F. (2005). A bibliometric analysis of 30 years of research and theory on corporate social responsibility and corporate social performance. *Business and Society, 44*(3), 283–317.

European Commission. (2011). Communication from the Commission to the European Parliament, the Council, the European Economic and Social Committee and the Committee of the Regions. A Renewed EU Strategy 2011–14 for Corporate Social Responsibility, No. COM (2011) 681, Brussels. http://eur-lex.europa.eu/legal-content/EN/TXT/?uri=COM:2011:0681:FIN. Accessed 24 September 2020.

Fox, T., Ward, H., & Howard, B. (2002). *Public sector roles in strengthening corporate social responsibility: A baseline study* (Report). The World Bank. https://pubs.iied.org/16017IIED/. Accessed 23 September 2020.

Hawrysz, L., & Foltys, J. (2016). Environmental aspects of social responsibility of public sector organizations. *Sustainability, 8*(1), 19.

Jonker, J. (2012). *New business models: An exploratory study of changing transactions creating multiple value(s)* (Working Paper). Radboud University Nijmegen, Nijmegen School of Management.

Marchetti, M., & Raudma, T. (Eds.). (2010). *Stocktaking 10 years of "Women in Science" policy by the European Commission 1999–2009*. Luxembourg: Publications Office of the European Union.

Pauzuoliene, J., & Mauriciene, I. (2013). Implementation of social responsibility in public institutions. *Socialiniai Tyrimai, 4*(33), 141–151.

Sangle, S. (2010). Critical success factors for corporate social responsibility: A public sector perspective. *Corporate Social Responsibility and Environmental Management, 17*, 205–214.

Štreimikienė, D., & Pušinaitė, R. (2009). The role of public sector in corporate social responsibility development in Lithuania. *Ekonomika, 86*, 55–67.

Ward, H. (2004). *Public sector roles in strengthening corporate social responsibility: Taking stock* (Report). The World Bank. https://pubs.iied.org/pdfs/16014IIED.pdf. Accessed 23 September 2020.

CHAPTER 2

The University Social Responsibility Framework by the International Federation of Catholic Universities: A Case of "Intelligent" Co-creation

Montserrat Alom Bartrolí

INTRODUCTION

This chapter presents an analysis of the collective process by which the International Federation of Catholic Universities (IFCU) produced a Framework for University Social Responsibility (USR) addressed to Catholic universities, with the aim to counterbalance the importance given nowadays to rankings that are mainly based on scientific performance.

Stress is placed on the two main challenges posed by the construction of an international USR Framework (named "the Newman Framework" after the Federation's Patron Saint, Cardinal John Henry Newman) and an Evaluation system relying on it. On the one hand, the lack of consensus

M. Alom Bartrolí (✉)
International Federation of Catholic Universities, Paris, France
e-mail: montserrat.alom@bureau.fiuc.org

L. Tauginienė and R. Pučėtaitė (eds.), *Managing Social Responsibility in Universities*, https://doi.org/10.1007/978-3-030-70013-3_2

7

about the meaning to be associated with the concept of USR, which has received multiple definitions and interpretations following actors' representations. On the other hand, difficulties encountered when seeking to build an international tool that may be applied locally in any part of the world despite national or regional specificities.

We will present the project's genesis and results in a chronological manner, while highlighting the strategies deployed to construct a benchmarking framework likely to encounter a high degree of consensus and an assessment system that can be applied in any context.

The project's two phases are analysed through the lens of the actor-network theory (ANT). The co-construction phase leading to the USR Framework includes 160 indicators and 20 criteria sorted into 4 main areas. The implementation phase leading to the Evaluation System relies on an innovative approach based on artificial intelligence (AI).

The chapter is written by one of the individuals involved in the project, namely its leader. In the following pages, the author's personal point of view is left aside in favour of a sociological posture that has been defined as "the intention of objectivity" (Hughes, 1996). Although there is no single recipe for objectivity when it comes to the observer-observed phenomenon dialectic, we acknowledge that the best resources are permanent awareness and self-criticism of the close relationship that exists in such cases (Morin, 1968). The following analysis, which relies, as well, on the examination of some project's materials and various types of documentation stemming from interactions, has therefore been conducted with a constant concern for reflexivity with regard to the field.

Going back to the project after its completion in a more reflective way allows for highlighting the challenges posed by the adoption of USR in an academic setting, and for better understanding the dynamics governing innovative co-creation processes that take place at the international level.

THEORETICAL AND CONCEPTUAL APPROACH

The ANT provides us with a theoretical and conceptual framework that allows for shedding some light on the process leading to the co-construction of a new consensual knowledge object (i.e., the Newman framework and evaluation system) in the field of USR.

According to this theory, actor-networks build hybrid networks that bring together both human and non-human entities as well as institutions, agencies, and all kinds of other actors, creating spaces of resources exchange and circulation mediated by social and cultural, as well as natural, material and technical interactions (Fenwick & Edwards, 2012). Actor-networks aim at establishing strong relationships with each of the entities deemed essential to reach a given purpose (Vinck, 2007).

The actors structuring research networks "are rather oriented towards strategic behaviours" defined as "the deliberate search for favourable positions in the network (that is to say, advantageous from the point of view of the actor), while being confronted with other actors who strive to achieve the same goal" (Latour, 1992, p. 61). These networks combine heterogeneous elements like "inscriptions (and in particular statements), technical devices, human actors (researchers, technicians, industrialists, politicians) and organizations (companies, charities, public agencies) interacting with each other" (Callon, Latour, & Akrich, 2006, pp. 239–240).

The concept of translation of others' interests or, in other words, actors' mobilization so that they follow the desired direction, is central to the ANT and requires incessant strategic work (Callon, 1986). In a paradigmatic case, Callon (1986) identified certain stages characterizing translation: first, *problematization*, which involves identifying an issue and all the actors concerned; second, *interessement* operations, which are strategies aiming at influencing other actors' interests and seal alliances with them; third, *enrolment*, which entails giving a specific role to the actors having joined the network; and, fourth, becoming legitimate *spokespersons* on behalf of other entities.

As for *interessement* operations intended to transform potential allies' interests, they may take varied forms like "pure and simple force", "seduction" or "mere solicitation" (Callon, 1986, p. 187). The same may include communication campaigns (online, audio-visual or through printed materials), on-site visits, joint meetings, negotiation processes, awards, and others. ANT also allows us to understand the process through which specific knowledge objects like the Newman framework and evaluation system may emerge, evolve and, finally, become durable. These objects, which stem out of interactions and negotiations involving human and non-human entities, may end up acquiring durable features that make them largely accepted. The objects become *black-boxed* when the complex process leading to their creation is set aside and their nature is not questioned any more (Latour, 1999).

ANT appears to be a relevant theoretical and conceptual approach for the analysis of the project selected as a case study and of the responses provided by the promoting organisation to reach the established goals.

UNDERSTANDING THE CONTEXT

Higher education (HE) general context today seems to be caught amidst two main contending trends: on the one hand, the dominance of rankings (like the *Times Higher Education* or the *Shanghai Ranking*), and narrowly-defined scientific criteria to evaluate higher education institutions (HEI), researchers and the academic community as a whole (Beigel, 2013); on the other hand, growing efforts to put forward values, meaning and responsibility in HE, which are giving rise to alternative evaluation systems (Alom & Mabille, 2020). Aligning on this second trend, the notion of responsibility is taking momentum in different areas across the academic world.

Apprehending University Social Responsibility

The multiple meanings associated with the concept of USR in the scholarly literature (Gaete Quezada, 2011) as well as the manifold representations that actors may have about it (Cunha Bastos, Barbosa de Souza, & Hoffmann, 2019) are essential to understand the challenges posed to the project examined.

As a reminder, the concept stems from the notion of corporate social responsibility (CSR), which first originated in the business sector. CSR aligned on the criteria of the ISO26000 standard, which provides guidelines for evaluation in seven core subjects: organisational governance, human rights, labour practices, the environment, fair operating practices, consumer issues, community involvement and development (ISO, 2018).

USR is said to be a variation of CSR adapted to the HEI context (Cunha Bastos et al., 2019). According to Carroll (1991), CSR involves society's expectations about the economic, legal, ethical and philanthropic aspects of organizations. Still, Benedicto, Maciel Stieg, Pallos Benedicto, and Rodrigues Lames (2012) state that CSR goes well beyond legal obligations and philanthropy as it involves a change of attitude. In the for-profit world, we can already find a wide range of definitions attached to the concept of corporate social responsibility; for instance, Dahlsrud (2008) identified 37 different definitions.

Similarly, the translation of CSR into the HE field has given rise to numerous variants (Esfijani, Hussain, & Chang, 2013), mainly due to such a heritage, to the emergence of regional approaches and to universities' specificities (Amorim et al., 2008). First, HEI are mission-oriented organisations, which are not only (or essentially) led by for-profit objectives; second, they possess a series of essential and unique features that make them quite different from any regular company. The core functions they are due to perform are synthetized in the so-called "three missions", that is, teaching, research and service to community (Molas-Gallart & Castro-Martínez, 2007). These missions, which are universities' *raison d'être*, account for substantial differences between this sector and other sectors in society.

Over the past years, authors studying USR have chosen to concentrate on different dimensions, audiences, or targets. Kliksberg (2009) stresses the ethical dimension of USR by emphasizing institutional efforts to go beyond legal or administrative duties and develop a strong ethical commitment towards society. Vallaeys, De la Cruz, and Sasia (2009) single out the role of stakeholders in the analysis and evaluation of USR impacts. More generally, Gaete Quezada (2011) establishes a typology that classifies the existing theories and approaches into three main groups, namely managerial, transformative and regulatory. The lack of a single approach in the understanding and operationalization of USR poses a main challenge in particular to the universities' strategic management (Gaete Quezada, 2011). Narrow attitudes towards responsibility as part of the university's missions may also affect effective development (Tauginienė & Mačiukaitė-Žvinienė, 2013), as well poor articulation between the principles stated and universities' strategic plans (Gaete Quezada & Alvarez Rodríguez, 2019). Moreover, it appears difficult to institutionalize USR activities because their implementation takes place in a fragmented and scattered manner (Vieira, Parisotto, & Ramos, 2018).

The 1990s saw the emergence of various initiatives and events promoted by HE actors in line with USR or associated aspects. Hence the founding of the Talloires Network in 1990, an international association promoting civic values and social responsibility in HE, which is composed of more than 400 member institutions today. The *World Declaration of Higher Education for the Twenty-First Century* (UNESCO, 1998) stressed the key role of universities within society, while a research project conducted by the Council of Europe between 1996 and 2000 focused on HEI's potential contribution to fostering the sense of citizenship in Europe (Plantan, 2002). More recently, the 2009 World Higher Education Conference organized by the United Nations Educational, Scientific and Cultural Organization (UNESCO) explored the new dynamics governing HE as a driver for societal change and development

(UNESCO, 2009). UNESCO also created a Regional Observatory on Social Responsibility for Latin America and the Caribbean (ORSALC), which conducted a study to determine the degree of social responsibility within the HEI of the region, while the United Nations Academic Impact Programme (UNAI) adopted as its motto "sharing a culture of intellectual social responsibility". Within Horizon 2020 the European Union (EU) started to promote the concept of "responsible research and innovation" (RRI), which was somehow enlarged by UNESCO's adoption of the *Recommendation on Science and Scientific Researchers* in 2017 (UNESCO, 2017). Pedagogical approaches like service-learning, which bring together education and service to society, are also taking momentum, not only in Europe, with, for example, the creation of the European Observatory of Service-Learning in Higher Education (EOSLHE), but also internationally, with the creation of UNISERVI-TATE, a network promoting service-learning among Catholic HEI across the world. Within the EU context, the EU-USR Project was the first one to propose a framework for USR based on the ISO26000 standard and other relevant resources (Amorim et al., 2008).

Although definitions and approaches abound and differ from one region to another, some recent work on USR tends to associate USR with social engagement, the so-called "third mission" of universities, which connects USR to actions having societal impact (CIRAD-IFCU, 2008). This is witnessed by various reports prepared by the Global University Network for Innovation (GUNI), an association devoted to strengthening the role of higher education within society (GUNI, 2009, 2014, 2017), or recent academic events like the 2019 European Association for Quality Assurance in Higher Education (ENQA) Conference held in Berlin, Germany, which focused on the societal engagement of universities, or else governmental approaches like Taiwan's recent policies for resource allocation based on the universities' degree of social engagement. Most IFCU members also tend to identify USR with the "third mission" of the university.

According to the Lebanese scholar Rizkallah (2017), there is often confusion between "university social responsibility" and the idea of "serving society" (i.e. "universities' third mission"); university social responsibility is a broader and deeper concept based on various principles and values related to the university's social role in teaching, research, governance, partnerships and other processes and activities. It involves responding to the needs of different types of stakeholders by promoting, among others, "social equality, sustainable development, individual dignity and freedom, respect for cultural diversity, support for human rights, and civil responsibility."

In brief, the lack of consensus regarding the aspects USR covers posed a serious challenge to the implementation and management of the project presented here. As we will see further on, the approach adopted by IFCU matches the Lebanese scholar's remarks.

Brief Overview of IFCU and the USR Project

IFCU is an organisation that brings together more than two hundred Catholic universities throughout the world for the purpose of intellectual, human and social progress (Aparicio Gómez & Tornos Curbillo, 2014). In its founding documents, IFCU defines itself as a "network of networks" (Valdrini, 2010, p. 164).

While at the international level there are many associations bringing together universities, IFCU is the only one that gathers Catholic universities from all continents, all religious orders combined. The Catholic identity of the members is highlighted in the founding documents of the Federation, as well as in the texts relating to its primary mission (Valdrini, 2010).

IFCU is headquartered in Paris, where its permanent Secretariat is located, although it has Regional Associations (like delegations) in each main region of the world. The staff at the headquarters is attached to one of the Federation's four departments, namely: the Training Department, the Foresight Unit, the International Advocacy Department, and the International Centre for Research and Decision Support (CIRAD).[1] The project examined here falls within the framework of the latter's activities.

Indeed, on October 2017, IFCU, through CIRAD, launched a three-year project aiming at creating a common reference framework on USR for Catholic universities, which joined international efforts to counterbalance growing competitive trends in HE while capitalizing on youngsters' said quest for meaning and Catholic universities' reflection on their identity's added value. This initiative stemmed out from the fact that the few existing initiatives in terms of frameworks and assessment guidelines "are often deficient, sectoral, or far too restricted" or else lack development

---

[1] See the Federation's website for further details: www.fiuc.org.

and dissemination (Alom & Mabille, 2020, p. 7). This situation leads Catholic universities to "invent independently or navigate between several systems in order to try to assess their USR policies and practices" (Alom & Mabille, 2020, p. 9).

According to the funded proposal, the new reference framework for USR assessment would (Alom & Mabille, 2020):

- Provide increased visibility for responsible policies and practices within Catholic universities;
- Encourage IFCU affiliates to improve their socially mindful policies and practices;
- Promote a global approach that allows for articulating a set of policies and practices that tend to be fragmented within universities;
- Contribute to positioning Catholic universities as social and societal actors that are responsible for their immediate environment while providing broader citizenship education on global issues;
- Identify good practices that could be inspiring for other Catholic universities;
- Build a realistic alternative to current university ranking systems.

Among the final goals, the project sought to provide Catholic HEI with a new type of positioning in the international university market by highlighting responsible policies and practices that had so far been quite neglected by the HE community.

ANALYSING USR PROJECT MANAGEMENT STRATEGIES AND RESULTS

Project management strategies and results are analysed chronologically by placing emphasis on the challenges linked to the notion of USR and on matching international standards and local requirements. The project took a two-stage approach, with a first phase oriented towards developing a USR Reference framework and a second one focused on building an Assessment system.

First Phase: The Co-construction of a Common Reference Tool Around the Notion of USR

Like most research and development projects, the one we analyse here went through *problematization* before its launch. *Problematization* consists of identifying a specific problem and a set of essential actors so that the questions raised can be solved (Callon, 1986). Acting as an actor-network, IFCU started by identifying USR as a relevant topic for member universities, one that deserves promotion in the face of "an academic context which has become very competitive" (Alom & Mabille, 2020, p. 4). Indeed, many decisions within HEI are increasingly governed in accordance with the place they hold in well-known university rankings. Similarly, national governmental policies tend to allocate funding based on how well HEIs are classified year after year. However, rankings like the *Times Higher Education* or the *Shanghai Ranking* have received substantial criticism as they tend to favour a certain type of institution at the expenses of all the others. Numerous biases have been enumerated concerning language prevalence, research focus, publication choices and, more generally, the narrow and partisan approach that they take. Indeed, the criteria used in such rankings are said to vehiculate a discourse that reproduces hegemonic positions that benefit a small group of big players in the research field (Felt et al., 2013). The *Leiden Manifesto for Research Metrics* is an example of an initiative seeking to warn about the excessive importance given to statistics when evaluating research performance and the negative consequences that this attitude may entail (Hicks, Wouters, Waltman, De Rijcke, & Rafols, 2015).

After enquiring about the topic's potential, IFCU prepared a fund proposal and identified a potential fund provider. It is important to state here that IFCU's first proposal was not accepted as such by the targeted fund provider. The main misunderstanding was due to divergent ways of apprehending USR. According to ANT, topics do not possess an intrinsic interest, but the same depends on how successfully an appropriate context has been built to create a specific demand (Latour, 1995). Thus, IFCU reworked on the proposal by slightly changing its focus, which was enlarged, although preserving all its essential features. This episode shows that conducting successful *interessement* operations (i.e., actions aimed at gaining support) requires good knowledge about stakeholders' expectations and ability to speak their own language.

The identification of key allies is also part of the *problematization* phase. Hence the creation of a Scientific Committee composed of 17 scholars from different member universities from across the world (Australia, Belgium, Brazil, Chile, Colombia, Democratic Republic of Congo, France, Italy, Mexico, Portugal, Spain), which was asked to provide advice and input. The importance of the role of experts as "knowledge carriers" in sharing knowledge has been largely acknowledged (Sanchez, 2006). According to Mažeikienė (2019, p. 101): "experts have become an important resource for organizational learning in universities and in inter-institutional cooperation initiatives through projects and networks, where tacit and implicit personal knowledge of individuals is transformed into explicit and embedded organizational knowledge".

Work performed during this phase in collaboration with Committee members also showed that current evaluation systems in the field were deficient, partial, and/or unsuited to academic reality (Alom & Mabille, 2020). It further stressed the contribution that the production of an international independent evaluation tool would bring to the HE landscape.

To start building the Newman Reference framework, IFCU opted for a co-construction strategy, which involved seeking a key potential ally possessing the right expertise in the field of evaluation. IFCU partnered thus with an extra-financial rating agency that had substantial experience in assessing various kinds of HEI at an international level. This joint work involved a long negotiation process because the selected partner held a representation of USR fully based on CSR, while IFCU wished to produce a tool more specific to the HEI context.

In a quest for contextual relevance and support, the resulting reference framework was pilot tested at eight member universities, located in Europe (Italy, Spain), Latin America (Brazil, Mexico), Africa (Ivory Coast), Asia and the Middle East (India, Lebanon), and North America (United States). Following a co-construction strategy, IFCU also sent the framework to the 17 Scientific Committee members for feedback, each of which confronted the criteria and indicators selected with the reality of their own institution and context.

The pilot test and feedback from the Committee helped readjust the reference framework, basically by adding a new main field (Catholic institutional identity), but reducing the overall number of criteria and indicators to keep only the most relevant ones. While the initial version was made up of 3 main fields (governance management, environmental respect, social practices) and over 250 indicators, the final framework covered 4 main fields (institution's identity being the fourth one), around 20 criteria and 160 indicators (see Fig. 2.1). A guide entitled *A Reference Framework for Assessing University Social Responsibility: From Theory to Practice* (Alom & Mabille, 2020) was released to present in more detail the framework and the criteria selected.

In accordance with the SMART approach, which encourages the use of indicators that are Specific, Measurable, Attainable, Relevant and Timely, the Newman Reference Framework seeks to measure the existence of policies (e.g. plans, laws, conventions, agreements) and practices (e.g. activities conducted, facilities in place, operating schemes, integration of specific issues in the curricula, involvement of specific stakeholders) within HEI.

The Newman Reference Framework's starting point was the Global Compact's principles, which were further defined, adapted, and enriched. For instance, in the "Governance" area, criteria GOV1 concerns the promotion of the balance of power and the effectiveness of the HEI governance body, GOV2 covers the effectiveness of control and audit

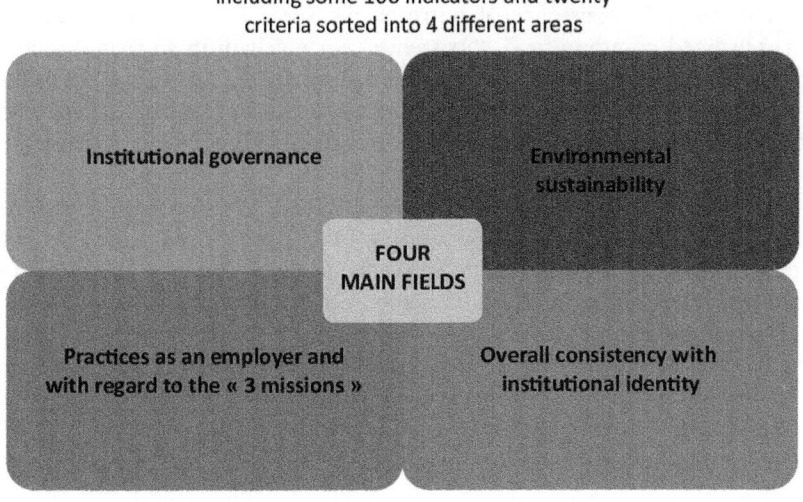

A result of a three-year collaboration endeavor including some 160 indicators and twenty criteria sorted into 4 different areas

Institutional governance

Environmental sustainability

FOUR MAIN FIELDS

Practices as an employer and with regard to the « 3 missions »

Overall consistency with institutional identity

Fig. 2.1 The IFCU Newman framework

systems, while GOV3 is dedicated to the prevention of fraud and corruption. Indicators associated to this area are, among others, the existence of mechanisms for students' consultation and representation, the existence of a mechanism to evaluate the governing body's performance, the discussion about topics related to USR in the Board or Committee meetings, a formalized commitment to the prevention of fraud and an alert system to trace cases of corruption.

Likewise, in the "Social practices" area (third major area of the Framework), eight criteria regard the university's activities as an employer (in other words, human resources), like SOC2, which is about preventing discrimination and promoting equal opportunities among employees, or SOC7, which covers measures oriented towards employees' skills, employability and career development. In this same major area, six criteria regard the university's "three missions": SOC9 "ensuring students' health and safety", SOC10 "respecting students' interests", SOC11 "promoting the economic and social development of local communities", SOC12 "promoting social responsibility in students' education", SOC13 "promoting social responsibility in research activities" and SOC14 "guaranteeing access to courses of study". Some indicators associated to these criteria are: "existence of formalized systems for collaborating with public authorities", "assessment of the social impact of activities carried out within society", "existence of outreach measures and activities targeting marginalized communities", "existence of a mechanism so that students participate in improving the content of syllabus", "existence of facilities to enhance wellness of students", "conduction of student satisfaction surveys", "research outcomes are disseminated beyond academia by different means".

In sum, the notion of USR finally adopted was broad and encompassing as it crosscut all the HEI policies and practices. It included CSR items, but went far beyond them. Indeed, areas that can be found in any type of organisation like governance, environmental efforts and social issues concerning employees and stakeholders were enriched by including two more fields: the "three missions" of the university and Catholic identity. Thus, a set of indicators was specifically defined to measure whether HEI teach their students in a responsible way while transmitting a series of values through their programmes, conduct research in a responsible manner, duly serve the community, and articulate responsibility and Catholic identity in a coherent way (Alom & Mabille, 2020).

The Newman Assessment System: An Innovative Artificial Intelligence-Based Evaluation Tool

The second phase of the project was particularly marked by the partnership that IFCU established with the Swiss GMAP Centre, an independent private think tank composed of an international and transdisciplinary team dedicated to analysing and forecasting changes in society. Its *enrolment*, that is, involvement with a specific role within the project network created by IFCU, made it possible to build an innovative assessment tool based on the new Reference Framework. The think tank had developed an advanced AI system of the machine-thinking type called Mileva. By favouring information's relevance rather than exhaustiveness, Mileva allows analysing complex situations and anticipating their evolution. It relies on the identification of a series of autonomous and heterogeneous agents that represent different elements of the world (e.g. issues, regulations, stakeholders) and interact following diverse behavioural models. Through the analysis of networks, behaviours, influence games and risks of rupture, Mileva provides thorough understanding of a given issue and insights on its most likely evolution in the three or four coming years.

Mileva, which "had proven itself many times to international organisations and renowned institutions" like, for instance, the Massachusetts Institute of Technology (MIT), the United Nations Security Council, the Geneva Centre for Security Policy or the Aga Khan Development Network, was employed in the project to implement the Newman assessment system: one that would use "artificial intelligence to provide neutral results, mindful of the different contexts universities find themselves in" and, in addition to measuring current USR performance, it would also "forecast future trends relevant to evaluated institutions" (Alom & Mabille, 2020, pp. 20–21).

The GMAP's *enrolment* contributed to take up the second main challenge faced by the project, that is, evaluating universities' USR performance in a way that is both unbiased and relevant for any context. Indeed, the implementation of an international standard at a local level cannot take place automatically, but it rather needs substantial adjustments. International cooperation organisations working in the educational and scientific field have reproduced post-colonial schemes for many years when addressing Southern countries (Gaillard, 1999). At a time, cooperation was mainly provided in the form of technical assistance wherein Northern experts travelled to the South to help "less skilled and equipped" peers

(Koch & Weingart, 2016). The way in which North-South cooperation is implemented today continues to be a touchy issue for international organizations like IFCU, 60% of whose members are located in Southern countries.

At the same time, producing standards that can be valid regardless of the socioeconomic, cultural and political context has always been challenging and launches the old debate about how to apprehend and connect local and global actions so that global aspects do not override local differences. If both dimensions have been long perceived as mutually exclusive, sociologist Robertson (1995), who is said to have coined the term of glocalisation, considers that, actually, the global cannot exclude the local. Similarly, ANT has shown that these are intertwined and interdependent dimensions as actions always have a situated character; they can only become global through the creation of networks composed of a number of actors that are situated in different settings (Ferrary & Callon, 2006). Overall, AI applied to assess universities' performance seemed to offer the best option to avoid transferring Western-based models that reproduce post-colonial schemes and to get nuanced results for each institution.

Although the indicators included in the Reference Framework are meant to be universal and adapted to most types of contexts, sociocultural, political, economic, historical, or religious aspects may account for differences in terms of relevance from one institution and country to another. When building the evaluation system, the issue of weighting indicators raised many questions as different levels of relevance had to be considered. For instance, if a university only welcomes female students, indicators regarding gender balance will not provide much useful information. Similarly, if indicators related to freedom to join trade unions appear as very relevant for some countries, for those where trade unions are hardly present such indicators will be far less relevant. AI's added value resides in the fact that it offers a tailor-made solution: it weights each of the indicators contained in the Newman reference framework depending on the institutional and geographical context of the evaluated HEI.

We can see here that USR is challenging, not only because of the diverse meanings associated with it, but also because of the different contexts of practice and development, both institutional and geographic. It should also be noted that, whereas the use of AI in the HE field is a current growing trend, it is the first time than an organisation applies it to evaluate universities' performance.

The resulting Newman Assessment System, which is open to any Catholic HEI recognized by the Congregation for Catholic Education, either IFCU member or not, is thus structured around one evaluation campaign per year, from April 1st to August 31st. Evaluation takes place through an online platform featuring the Newman reference framework's indicators, which are formulated as questions to which universities have to answer; HEI are also required to provide documents in support of their answers. AI contributes to completing questions left unanswered while comparing and qualifying all the data and documentation provided as a part of the analysis.

Every institution's results are concentrated in an interactive dashboard featuring the percentage of compliance with USR standards for each of the 4 main fields defined (governance, environment, social practices, identity). The dashboard allows each HEI to gain understanding of both current scores and expected ones, while providing recommendations for improvement and warning about future risks. It also shows the world and regional average scores so that HEI can better position themselves with regard to others.

The Newman Assessment System grants up to four USR accreditation labels, one for each of the main areas covered by the evaluation: the USR Governance label, the USR Environment label, the USR Social Practices label and the USR Identity label. The granting of the labels, which are valid for a period of 3 years, is conditional on obtaining threshold scores: a one-star label for a score between 35 and 49%, a two-star label for a score between 50 and 74%, a three-star label for a score of 75% or higher. A score below 35% does not entitle to a label in the field concerned.[2] Although IFCU may display the names of labelled universities on its site or communication materials, it undertakes not to present evaluated HEI in the form of a ranking or any similar classification. The latter would be contrary to the project's spirit, which aimed precisely at countering excessive attention to rankings.

During this second phase, IFCU also reflected about the best ways to attract member universities to apply for an evaluation. In addition to relying on the award of accreditation labels, it identified key allies that could help to implement a successful communication strategy. It thus invited Regional Associations (which are the Federation's branches

---

[2] Detailed information on the Newman Assessment System can be find on: http://www.fiuc.org/article10_en.html.

in each region of the world) to present the Newman system in their respective places. IFCU mobilization strategy also involved using varied media supports (promotional video, articles in electronic journals, free online webinars, press releases, emailing, organisation's e-newsletters and website) and ensuring presence in different social networks (namely Facebook and LinkedIn).

As the first evaluation campaign of this newly-created system has not started, yet, results in terms of number of universities evaluated and labels granted are not available, but attracting HEI to apply for evaluation is a continuous time-consuming task, which requires substantial investment and fine-tuning strategies. It also involves keeping away contestation about the system created. As put forward by ANT, when the objects become black-boxed a step forward is made in that they are unlikely to be questioned or criticized. Still, getting recognition from all the actors that belong to the HE world over time is not an easy task, particularly in the face of rapidly changing contemporary societies. That is the reason why IFCU reserved the right to modify both the framework and the assessment system in accordance with major social transformations. The initiative's success will ultimately depend on the effectiveness of the actions conducted to attract universities and the system's capacity to adapt to evolutions in HE and the society as a whole.

CONCLUSION

We have analysed an international project aiming at creating: first, a framework that embeds a USR definition broadly accepted by HEI worldwide and, second, an assessment system that allows for evaluating the same set of policies and practices in different institutional and regional contexts in a tailored manner.

Unlike most authors that tend to examine USR understanding and implementation in selected HEI, we have rather placed our focus on an organization that represents HEI from different regions of the world. Our analysis integrates two of the main challenges that are posed by USR nowadays, namely, the lack of a consensual definition, which is accompanied by a considerable number of representations among HE actors, and the difficulties linked to measuring USR performance in different academic settings, which tend to keep USR policies and practices invisible and therefore undervalued by the HE community.

As the construction of the Newman Reference Framework and Assessment System is quite recent, we lack data to measure its degree of success. Still, the creation of an evaluation system that may be effectively applied in any Catholic HEI in the world and that ensures both institutional and contextual relevance thanks to the use of AI makes it an unprecedented evaluation initiative in the HE field.

While adding to the rising number of activities that seek to promote values and principles based on moral, civic or engaged positions, this initiative hopes to counterbalance HE competitive-led dynamics and open up avenues for realistic and effective alternatives to current rankings.

REFERENCES

Alom, M., & Mabille, F. (2020). *A reference framework for assessing university social responsibility: From theory to practice*. Paris: CIRAD-IFCU.

Amorim, J. P., Burgos, D., Arenas, B., Borcos, A., Carrasco, A., De Carvalho, L. X., Coimbra, J. L., Dima, G., Freires, T., Loja, E., Martin, B., Menezes, I., Negaides, A., Osuna López, M. C., Robles, M., Rodrigues, F., & Marjolein Don, R. (2008). *University social responsibility: A common European reference framework. Final public report of the EU-USR project, February 2015, 52709--LLP--2012-1-RO-ERASMUS-ESIN*. Brussels: EACEA. http://www.eu-usr.eu/wp-content/uploads/2015/04/D1.4-Final-Report-Public-Part-EN.pdf. Accessed 25 February 2020.

Aparicio Gómez, R., & Tornos Curbillo, A. (2014). *Les cultures des jeunes dans les universités catholiques: Une étude mondiale*. Paris: CCR-FIUC.

Beigel, F. (2013). Centros y periferias en la circulación internacional del conocimiento. *Nueva Sociedad, 245*, 110–123.

Benedicto, S. C., Maciel Stieg, C., Pallos Benedicto, E., & Rodrigues Lames, E. (2012). Ações de responsabilidade social versus estratégias empresariais: Estudo multicaso em instituições financeiras públicas e privadas. *Revista Symposium, 10*, 20–39.

Callon, M. (1986). Éléments pour une sociologie de la traduction: La domestication des coquilles Saint-Jacques et des marins-pêcheurs dans la baie de Saint-Brieuc. *L'Année Sociologique, 36*, 169–208.

Callon, M., Latour, B., & Akrich, M. (2006). *Sociologie de la traduction: Textes fondateurs*. Paris: Presses de l'Ecole des Mines.

Carroll, A. B. (1991). The pyramid of corporate social responsibility: Toward the moral management of organizational stakeholders. *Business Horizons, 34*(4), 39–48. https://doi.org/10.1016/0007-6813(91)90005-G.

CIRAD-IFCU. (2008). *Crossviews on Catholic university social responsibility*. Paris: IFCU.

Cunha Bastos, F. C., Barbosa de Souza, M. J., & Hoffmann, E. M. (2019). University social responsibility: An analysis from the Carroll's model. *Revista de Negócios, 24*(3), 27–48.

Dahlsrud, A. (2008). How corporate social responsibility is defined: An analysis of 37 definitions. *Corporate Social Responsibilty and Environmental Management, 15*(1), 1–13. https://doi.org/10.1002/csr.132.

Esfijani, A., Hussain, F., & Chang, E. (2013). University social responsibility ontology. *Engineering Intelligent Systems, 21*(4), 271–281.

Felt, U., Barben, D., Irwin, A., Joly, P. B., Rip, A., Stirling, A., & Stöckelová, T. (2013). *Science in society: caring for our futures in turbulent times.* Science policy brief, 50. Strasbourg: European Science Foundation.

Fenwick, T., & Edwards, R. (2012). Introduction. In T. Fenwick & R. Edwards (Eds.), *Researching education through actor-network theory* (pp. ix–xxii). London: Wiley-Blackwell.

Ferrary, M., & Callon, M. (2006). Les réseaux sociaux à l'aune de la théorie de l'acteur-réseau. *Sociologies Pratiques, 2*(13), 37–44. https://doi.org/10.3917/sopr.013.0037.

Gaete Quezada, R. (2011). La responsabilidad social universitaria como desafío para la gestión estratégica de la educación superior: El caso de España. *Revista de Educación, 355,* 109–133.

Gaete Quezada, R., & Alvarez Rodríguez, J. (2019). Responsabilidad social universitaria en Latinoamérica. *Los casos de URSULA y AUSJAL. Revista Actualidades Investigativas en Educación, 19*(3), 1–27. https://doi.org/10.15517/aie.v19i3.38637.

Gaillard, J. (1999). *La coopération scientifique et technique avec les pays du Sud: Peut-on partager la science?.* Paris: Karthala.

GUNI Higher Education in the World Reports 1-3. (2009). *Higher education at a time of transformation: New dynamics for social responsibility.* Basingstoke, UK: Palgrave Macmillan.

GUNI Higher Education in the World 5. (2014). *Knowledge, engagement and higher education: Contributing to social change.* Basingstoke, UK: Palgrave Macmillan.

GUNI Higher Education in the World 6. (2017). *Towards a socially responsible university: Balancing the global with the local.* Girona: GUNI. http://www.guninetwork.org/files/download_full_report.pdf. Accessed 15 September 2020.

Hicks, D., Wouters, P., Waltman, L., De Rijcke, S., & Rafols, I. (2015). The Leiden Manifesto for research metrics. *Nature, 520,* 429–431. https://doi.org/10.1038/520429a.

Hughes, E. C. (1996). *Le regard sociologique : Textes rassemblés et présentés par J.-M. Chapoulie.* Paris: Editions de l'EHESS.

ISO. (2018). *ISO26000 guidance on social responsibility: Discovering ISO26000.* Geneva: International Organization for Standardization. https://www. iso.org/files/live/sites/isoorg/files/store/en/PUB100258.pdf. Accessed 17 September 2020.

Kliksberg, B. (2009). Los desafíos éticos pendientes en un mundo paradojal: El rol de la universidad. *Revista del CLAD Reforma y Democracia, 43,* 63–82.

Koch, S., & Weingart, P. (2016). *The delusion of knowledge transfer: The impact of foreign aid experts on policy-making in South Africa and Tanzania.* Cape Town: African Minds.

Latour, B. (1992). *Les réseaux que la raison ignore.* Paris: L'Harmatttan.

Latour, B. (1995). *Le métier de chercheur: Regard d'un anthropologue.* Paris: INRA.

Latour, B. (1999). *Pandora's hope: Essays on the reality of science studies.* Cambridge, MA: Harvard University Press.

Mažeikienė, N. (2019). Understanding the evolution of service learning at European universities: Insights from actor-network theory. In P. Aramburuzabala, L. McIlrath, & H. Opazo (Eds.), *Embedding service learning in European higher education: Developing a culture of civic engagement* (pp. 93–108). London, New York: Routledge.

Molas-Gallart, J., & Castro-Martínez, E. (2007). Ambiguity and conflict in the development of 'Third Mission' indicators. *Research Evaluation, 16*(4), 321–330. https://doi.org/10.3152/095820207X263592.

Morin, E. (1968). Pour une sociologie de la crise. *Communications, 12,* 2–16. https://doi.org/10.3406/comm.1968.1168.

Plantan, F. (2002). *Universities as sites of citizenship and civic responsibility. Final general report for the Council of Europe.* https://rm.coe.int/16807465ad. Accessed 16 September 2020.

Rizkallah, S. (2017). Fondements et principes du concept de la responsabilité sociale des universités. *L'Orient-Le Jour.* https://www.lorientlejour.com/art icle/1061240/fondements-et-principes-du-concept-de-la-responsabilite-soc iale-des-universites.html. Accessed 20 May 2020.

Robertson, R. (1995). Glocalisation: Time-space and homogeneity-heterogeneity. In M. Featherstone, R. Robertson, & S. Lash (Eds.), *Global modernities* (pp. 25–44). London, Thousand Oaks: Sage.

Sanchez, R. (2006). Knowledge management and organizational learning: Fundamental concepts for theory and practice. In B. Renzl, K. Matzler, & H. H. Hinterhuber (Eds.), *The future of knowledge management* (pp. 29–61). London: Palgrave Macmillan.

Tauginienė, L., & Mačiukaitė-Žvinienė, S. (2013). Managing university social responsibility. *Journal of Humanities and Social Science, 13*(4), 84–91.

UNESCO. (1998). *Higher education in the twenty-first century: Vision and action: World conference.* Paris: UNESCO.

UNESCO. (2009, July 5–8). *Communiqué. 2009 World Conference on Higher Education: The new dynamics of higher education and research for societal change and development.* Paris: UNESCO. https://unesdoc.unesco.org/ark:/48223/pf0000183277. Accessed 14 September 2020.

UNESCO. (2017). *Recommendation on science and scientific researchers.* Paris: UNESCO. https://unesdoc.unesco.org/ark:/48223/pf0000260889. page=116. Accessed 10 September 2020.

Valdrini, P. (2010). La Fédération Internationale des Universités Catholiques à travers ses Statuts. *Transversalités, 4*(116), 151–165.

Vallaeys, F., De la Cruz, C., & Sasia, P. M. (2009). *Responsabilidad social universitaria. Manual de primeros pasos.* Mexico D.F.: McGraw Hill.

Vieira, C. C. N., Parisotto, I. R. D. S., & Ramos, S. P. (2018). Responsabilidade social universitária: Um estudo sobre seu significado para os representantes dos grupos de interesse de uma universidade. *Revista de Negócios, 23*(4), 7–24.

Vinck, D. (2007). *Sciences et société: Sociologie du travail scientifique.* Paris: Armand Colin.

CHAPTER 3

(Re-)Constructing Measurement of University Social Responsibility

Loreta Tauginienė and Raminta Pučėtaitė

INTRODUCTION

The social responsibility of organisations, be they private, public or non-governmental, has been on the agenda of supranational political documents, regulations and standards (e.g. ISO26000, Paris Agreement, UN Sustainable Development Goals), national agreements and initiatives as well as stakeholders' expectations regarding organisational activities which have an impact on present and future generations (Baur & Schmitz, 2013; Brundlandt, 1987; European Commission, 2011). These developments set higher demands for institutional social and/or environmental performance and, respectively, accountability, but disregard institutional mission due to unchanging criteria (Borden, Coates, & Bringle, 2018), may differ from reality due to the focus on opinions (subjectivity) or are

L. Tauginienė (✉)
Hanken School of Economics, Helsinki, Finland
e-mail: loreta.tauginiene@hanken.fi

R. Pučėtaitė
Kaunas Faculty, Vilnius University, Vilnius, Lithuania
e-mail: raminta.pucetaite@knf.vu.lt

not legally binding (Turker, 2018a), miss to measure outcomes (impacts) or are insufficiently enforced by different stakeholders or institutions. These demands are met by a few broad and specific certification and/or reporting guidelines and standards, such as the UN Global Compact, Global Reporting Initiative, Social Accountability 8000, U-Map and Assessment of Higher Education Learning Outcomes, which, like any standard solution, require more sophistication and a wider scope. In this respect, higher education as a service industry mostly in public sector meets its own challenges, e.g. how should higher education institutions such as universities respond to societal expectations for public good as key public service providers and consumers in line with their identity and development perspectives (e.g. Albert & Whetten, 1985; Herrera & Sánchez, 2017; Winter & O'Donohue, 2012; Young, Nagpal, & Adams, 2016). Through the specific activities such as teaching, research and community engagement (e.g. De Boer, Enders, & Leisyte, 2007; Jongbloed, Enders, & Salerno, 2008) universities have an impact on different stakeholders on the one hand and experience tensions when coordinating these activities on the other hand (Krizek, Newport, White, & Townsend, 2012). Although, in contrast to private sector organisations where scandals are typically considered as a threat to reputation and are respectively managed, universities do not, as a rule, consider themselves accountable for social or environmental impact or put emphasis on sustainability or social responsibility as instruments for added value to themselves or their stakeholders (Adams, 2013; Young et al., 2016); their impact calls for changes in the sector. These changes should be addressed not only by introducing syllabi on social responsibility and/or sustainability, and social initiatives with communities, but also leading by example as well as benchmarking and improving their own organisational mission-based practices which play a crucial role in embedding sustainable development goals. Hence, the concept of university social responsibility (USR) should not only be operationalised but also suggest a set of indicators for measuring the duty of socialising and embedding institutional values as well as the quality of university governance and management, particularly when responsibly managing their specific activities in relation to various stakeholders (Ayala-Rodríguez, Barreto, Rozas Ossandón, Castro, & Moreno, 2019; Gómez, Pujols, Alvarado, & Vargas, 2018). On the one hand, such measurement will allow the modelling of comparable uniformities based on commonly agreed rules, testifying the prosocial role of universities and improving their social visibility through account-ability, transparency and good governance (Ayala-Rodríguez et al., 2019; Sauder & Espeland, 2009; Timmermans & Epstein, 2010). On the other hand, such measurement will leave space for case-based adaptations and a mission-oriented and value-driven approach to an organisation's responsibility management.

Studies on USR measurement and reporting have been in the spot-light of academic discussion over recent decades. A few models designated specifically to evaluate USR have been developed; however, each of them addresses different aspects. The frameworks mostly focus on the university-specific activity areas, such as teaching/learning, research, and engagement with society (Esfijani & Chang, 2012; Godínez Valdés, Santos, & Hernández, 2014; Noguera, Moncayo, & Martí-Vilar, 2014; Vallaeys, 2013; Vallaeys, De la Cruz, & Sasia, 2009; Viteri-Moya, Jácome-Villacres, & Medina-León, 2013), principles that guide university activities, such as openness, transparency, economic impact, engagement (Esfijani & Chang, 2012), or performance dimensions, such as educative, epistemic-cognitive, social, environmental and organisational performance (Aristimuño, 2012; Vallaeys et al., 2009). Lately, some studies have appeared on virtual USR in relation to academic reputation (Canelón, 2013; Esfijani & Chang, 2012). In addition, some corporate practices emerge to measure social responsibility in terms of how ethical values are embedded (Fray, 2007). These different approaches call for an inte-grative approach that facilitates management of USR, giving guidance to organisational development and positive impact on society. Despite these previous attempts, there is no consensus on how USR should be eval-uated in different institutional socio-cultural, i.e. authentic, contexts. In this regard, this chapter aims, based on previous studies, to develop a conceptually consolidated framework of USR that after critical appraisal integrates the above-mentioned dimensions of university activities and to test its construct validity with an expert survey.

Understanding University Social Responsibility

For a long time social responsibility has been associated with private companies (so-called corporate social responsibility [e.g. Carroll, 1979, 1999]) while to date it is acknowledged that the university as a social institution "needs <...> minimum morals" (García-Marzá, 2005, p. 215) and as any organisation has "a special responsibility to lead by example"

(Wigmore-Álvarez & Ruiz-Lozano, 2014, p. 1). Such amenability implies responsibilities towards diverse university stakeholders, particularly in relation to what and how a university performs and what drives a university to act in one way or another. Moreover, a university is expected to internalise its social responsibility through institutional values (Tauginienė & Urbanovič, 2018). In this chapter, we combine two main components of institutional social responsibility: a stakeholder-driven approach and institutional values. In line with this articulation, university social responsibility can be described as "a commitment towards performance based on ethical and other conventional principles that are respectively substantiated in the mission, values and related activities in the interplay with all possible stakeholders in order to create social value foremost" (Tauginienė & Urbanovič, 2018, p. 159). Given this definition, universities as providers of public services embody value-driven motives for engaging in socially responsible activities which lie in internal management systems driven by both internal and external factors (De Jong & Van der Meer, 2017; Groza, Pronschinske, & Walker, 2011; Sheehy, 2015; Turker, 2018b).

All universities claim their autonomy that accordingly implies a large space for acting at its discretion through taking responsibility and accountability in this regard. Given this, autonomy has been preserved in universities until today, while many other organisations had to shift their pattern because of (inter)national regulations (Fuller, 2005; Rinne & Koivula, 2005). Gburi (2015) argues that the preservation of autonomy (i.e. one of the core university institutional values) is possible once it is linked to values inherent to the market. By contrast, Rinne and Koivula (2005) question the long-lasting university autonomy due to the marketisation of higher education and research. They argue that regardless of how universities will transform, the need to manifest their social responsibility will always remain because of their impact on society.

Furthermore, to secure autonomy and legitimacy universities' practices are expected to meet the minimum standards prescribed by law. However, in terms of USR, universities are expected to demonstrate an integrity-based approach and commitment to stakeholders that go beyond compliance with externally imposed inter-organisational or legal requirements at all managerial levels. Therefore, although accountability and social or environmental reporting may be an expectation in some sociocultural contexts, it is not an all-case solution for creating value to the organisation and society.

Burke and Logsdon (1996) point out that institutional social responsibility should be foremost strategically oriented to such constituents as centrality, specificity, proactivity, voluntarism, and visibility that lead to value creation. However, these authors describe value creation as economic benefits which are deficient in universities. Universities, by their traditional nature and due to public management reforms (Pollitt & Bouckaert, 2000), are expected to put extra efforts to create social value through the promotion of the wellbeing of multiple stakeholders (Henkel, 1997), but still remain faithful to their institutional values (Rosenzweig, 1999–2000) and fulfil governance ethics in the university, between universities and other organisations, and between university and society (Wieland, 2001). Following this line, social responsibility in higher education, like in private sector, is getting recognition as a tool for university reputation risk management on the one hand (Stadler, Andrade dos Reis, Arantes, & Del Corso, 2017) and a guarantee for public trust in universities on the other hand (Leja, 2010; McDonald, 2009; McNay, 2007).

Revisiting University Social Responsibility Measurement Tools

In a broad sense, there have been a few attempts to measure value created by universities. Some of these attempts relate either to diagnostic self-assessment (e.g. to discover employee satisfaction, benefits of the product and service or one's evaluations on a course) or comparative self-assessment (e.g. Global Reporting Initiative at international scale) (Polese & Monetta, 2006). Others, such as the Times Higher Education World University Rankings, United Nations (UN) Principles for Responsible Management Education or accreditation labels (e.g. AACSB), which are principally used by business schools, focus on USR to a limited extent (e.g. interlinking with a few UN Sustainable Development Goals or applied to a certain discipline). These rather suggest indicators related to the assurance of education/research quality and impact on society, but might be still implicitly interconnected to USR. Another set of guidelines for measuring USR, particularly in Europe, may be derived from responsible research and innovation (RRI) indicators created by the European Commission funded project MoRRI (The evolution of Responsible Research and Innovation…, 2018). They offer five dimensions such as gender equality, science literacy and education, public engagement, open access, ethics, and governance with 36 indicators. The indicators relate to measuring USR, yet the framework predominantly relates to research and innovation activities which are expected to deliver competitive advantage to regions. However, in less developed countries a major part of university funding is related to teaching activities and therefore RRI may be disregarded in specific contexts. In any case, although the available frameworks give room for USR measurement to some extent, we cannot avoid the thought that USR might become a stunt, a marketing tool, rather than the genuine purport and expression of university real-life performance driven by the values-and-stakeholder rationale.

In this respect, a few malfunctions in dealing with these measurement challenges have been identified. First, using fuzzy logic-based approach, Esfijani and Chang (2012) state that a university should provide benefits instead of looking for profit, as it has responsibilities towards diverse stakeholders. By bearing these responsibilities, a university contributes to the quality of life of their stakeholders (Esfijani & Chang, 2012; Păunescu, Drăgan (Gilmeanu), & Găucă, 2017; Rodríguez & Hernández, 2017). For this purpose, Esfijani and Chang (2012) distil six criteria related to USR measurement: (1) teaching/learning; (2) engagement; (3) transparency; (4) outreach activities; (5) research activities; and (6) economic impact. Within these criteria social, ethical, and economic dimensions are considered. The proportion of these dimensions is uneven. For instance, truly little attention is paid to the ethical dimension of USR, while Wan-Jan (2006) states that social responsibility is both an ethical stance and an institutional strategy. Some studies on ethical virtues as indicators of ethical or virtuous organisations (Huhtala, Kangas, Kaptein, & Feldt, 2018; Kaptein, 2008, 2011; Pučėtaitė, Novelskaitė, Lämsä, & Riivari, 2016) add argument to the importance of the ethical dimension in the USR framework. In this sense, the intrinsic purpose of a university's existence resides in the university's legitimacy to embed its social role (Drori, Delmestri, & Oberg, 2016; Meyer, Ramirez, Frank, & Schofer, 2007; Păunescu et al., 2017).

Second, it is difficult to grasp the continuity and a long-term perspective or dynamics of USR development from the indicators suggested in the mentioned frameworks. In most cases, indicators are based on the fact of existence of the respective processes but lack a clear parallel with impact and change to trace the dynamics of USR development. Furthermore, studies present results of USR measurement as a baseline for further benchmarking and as a basis for revising and improving university effects.

Hence, in the proceeding sections we describe the process and results of integrating the available frameworks to address the gaps in the USR measurement discourse.

METHODOLOGICAL APPROACH

To develop an integrative framework of USR, we used the critical appraisal to select academic papers which comprehensively deal with USR measurement for further analysis. We found four papers that exhaustively suggest the USR dimensions (or impacts) and operationalise them (Table 3.1).

Based on these studies, we identified seven dimensions, namely, organisational, environmental, educational, economic, ethical, epistemic-cognitive, and social (Table 3.1) that encompass 24 unique items and 143 indicators.

Most of the selected papers explicitly align the USR dimensions with the items. However, although Vallaeys et al. (2009) identify USR dimensions, the authors fail to explicitly align them with the items suggested. Also, Esfijani and Chang (2012) fail to align the USR dimensions with 39 per cent of the items. As a result, the authors of this chapter attempt to assign the items to the related dimensions based on their long-lasting academic and administrative work experience and expert knowledge in the field (e.g. business ethics, corporate social responsibility) when building a set of potential indicators.

Besides, in the above papers, each dimension bearing the same name was differently defined. For example, Vallaeys et al. (2009) defined the cognitive dimension as a focus on research and teaching and the stance of such internal stakeholders as teaching staff and researchers, while Aristimuño (2012) described the same dimension as knowledge creation and production as well as science relevant to society. The same observation is applied to the economic dimension where variant descriptions were provided by Esfijani and Chang (2012) and Moneva Abadía and Vallespín (2012). These discrepancies prompted us to develop our own descriptions of each dimension to refine the existing ones and align them with the definition of USR we follow in this chapter.

In all, six dimensions have been crystallised in our set of dimensions: organisational, social, environmental, educational, ethical, and economic (Fig. 3.1 and Table 3.2). The cognitive dimension suggested by Aristimuño (2012) and Vallaeys et al. (2009) was excluded as redundant due to the overlap of its contents with those of the other dimensions, such

Table 3.1   USR dimensions from previous studies

Dimension (impact)	Brief description
Educational	Vallaeys et al. (2009): covers learning and addresses the stance of students
	Aristimuño (2012): defines curriculum subjects and projects that are designated to the solution of social issues
Organisational	Vallaeys et al. (2009): relates to managerial practice of labour and environment and addresses the stance of internal stakeholders, such as administrative staff, teaching staff and researchers
Environmental	Moneva Abadía and Vallespín (2012): relates to ecosystems (such as air, water, soil)
	Aristimuño (2012): demonstrates management actions to incorporate environmental aspects and related impacts; it shows the relationship of the university with its stakeholders (clients and internal and external suppliers) through ethnic, religious, gender and disability integration
Cognitive	Vallaeys et al. (2009): focuses on research and teaching and addresses the stance of internal stakeholders, such as teaching staff and researchers
	Aristimuño (2012): shows knowledge creation and production as well as science relevant to society
Social	Vallaeys et al. (2009): covers development, including transfer of knowledge and social campaigns. It addresses external stakeholders, such as business, public sector and others
	Esfijani and Chang (2012): ramifies into activities related to teaching, engagement, transparency, outreach, research and economic impact
	Moneva Abadía and Vallespín (2012): identifies social performance through human rights, labour conditions, and responsibility for outputs
	Aristimuño (2012): reveals the relationship with social actors through social development
Ethical	Esfijani and Chang (2012): ramifies into activities related to teaching, engagement, transparency, outreach, research, and economic impact
Economic	Esfijani and Chang (2012): ramifies into activities related to teaching, engagement, transparency, outreach, research, and economic impact
	Moneva Abadía and Vallespín (2012): relates to economic conditions of stakeholders and economic systems at local, national, and global levels

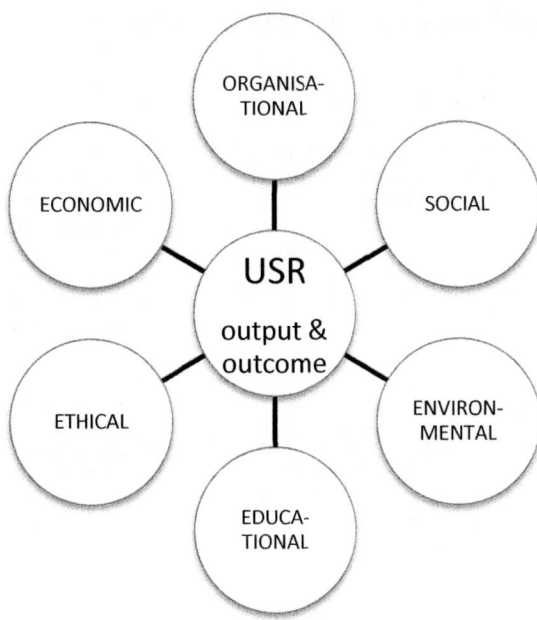

Fig. 3.1   Initial dimensions of an integrative framework of USR

as social and organisational. As an example, Aristimuño (2012) suggested an indicator "In the development programs or social projects other social actors and non-academic knowledge are incorporated" under a cognitive dimension which refers to our definition of a social dimension (outreach and social activities to (and with) internal and external stakeholders). The former refers to the processes designated to proclaim results achieved, but it does not testify results themselves.

As a typical practice of developing new instruments for social phenomena measuring (Thomas & Lucas, 2019), the coders (authors) used critical appraisal to score the relevance of indicators using a 3-point response scale where 1 denoted "highly recommended", 2—"somehow recommended" and 3—"not recommended". To maximise reliability (Denzin, 1970), both authors first carried out the coding independently and afterwards discussed their coding until they reached consensus. After the first round of coding independently a fair inter-coder agreement was reached, i.e. a full inter-coder agreement was nine per cent (13 out of

Table 3.2   Initial dimensions and related items of an integrative framework on USR

Dimension	Dimension definition	Items
Organisational	Inward managerial practices of labour in terms of internal stakeholders	Assurance of good institutional practices regarding equity and non-discrimination
		Participation of trade union representatives in decision making
		Transparency of elections at all governance and management levels
		Social commitment (e.g. volunteering; social networking)
		Communication of university social responsibility
Social	Outreach and social activities to (and with) internal and external stakeholders	Support for disadvantaged social groups
		Social relevance of research
		Fulfilment of workplace requirements
		Academic activism
Environmental	Environmental actions undertaken by and designated to internal stakeholders	Waste management
		Responsible consumption
		Purchases and acquisitions related to fair trade, environmental security
Educational	Learning and training activities delivered to internal and external stakeholders	Development of transdisciplinary skills
		Lifelong learning promotion
		Networking
Ethical	Embedding ethical practices within the university	Ethics infrastructure
		Communication
Economic	Economic conditions of internal stakeholders to demonstrate openness to society at large	Sustainability
		Transparency
		Responsiveness

143) while partial inter-coder agreement was 26% (37 out of 143). The partial inter-coder agreement denotes a double code by one of the authors where one of them overlaps with a code assigned by the other coder. Subsequently, to advance the inter-coder agreement on the interpretation of the dimensions, items and indicators and to deal with differences in

scoring, a discussion was carried out that resulted in completely omitting items with zero agreement and distilling 27 items (nine items and one unnamed item were unique) inherent to all dimensions. This discussion helped to intensify theoretical and practical sensitivity as well as to predict whether the indicators would be reliable, sensitive, specific, and feasible (Mainz, 2003; Rubin, Pronovost, & Diette, 2001). Afterwards ten unique items were refined into 20 items due to both certain recurrence of their content and over-saturated content (Table 3.2). For example, an item 'Recycling' was covered in two items, such as 'Waste management' and 'Responsible consumption' while an item 'Social participation' was interspersed in four items, such as 'Social commitment (e.g. volunteering; social networking)', 'Support for disadvantaged social groups', 'Social relevance of research' and 'Academic activism'. This refinement also resulted in including new overarching indicators according to the USR definition used in this chapter.

To refine the set of 20 pre-selected items containing 113 quantitative and qualitative indicators, we used purposeful sampling to select the most information-rich experts in USR and Corporate Social Responsibility (CSR) (Palinkas et al., 2015; Patton, 2002). Overall, we made a list of 22 national experts (16 females and 6 males) from nine research and higher education institutions and four business enterprises. Nine experts (eight women and one man) voluntarily agreed to take part in the refinement procedure and signed the informed consent. Their expert knowledge ranged from sustainability, environmental sustainability, business ethics, CSR through quality management, corporate sustainable innovation, RRI to corporate financial accountability, and energy efficiency. Seven experts represented the scientific sector while two experts represented the business sector. All experts published at least two studies in the field of social responsibility. Hence, the experts were asked to critically rate the meaning and the relevance of the indicators to the USR measurement using a 3-point response scale where 1 denoted "a very important indicator", 2—"somewhat important", 3—"not important at all" (Lawshe, 1975; Thomas & Lucas, 2019). The evaluative process was carried out online, independently, and anonymously. The experts could provide any comments on the indicators on each page of the online questionnaire. The experts expressed the combined judgement that allowed empirically testify both the meaning and relevance of the content of each item and its indicators (the content validation).

Four experts' comments on the indicators, which related to the their technical layout in the online survey, requested term definitions, and suggested change in the wording of the statements describing indicators, e.g. "alternative energy resources" was recommended to be changed to "renewable energy resources" (which we respectively did; Table 3.3). One expert suggested an additional indicator for a university's social responsibility to employees, e.g. s/he noted that the quantity and frequency of accidents at work may be not that significant as an indicator of USR, but insurance offered by a university as the employer may be. Despite this valuable comment, the latter indicator was not included by the authors in the list of the main indicators of USR measurement at this stage as public universities do not usually have a legal basis to act as insurance funds and, in contrast to private organisations, they do not have the funds to offer extra insurance as a benefit to the employee.

Furthermore, we proceeded with the calculation of content validity ratio (CVR) (Thomas & Lucas, 2019) to sort out the final set of valid USR indicators. We calculated the CVR based on the critical value applied to 9-experts' panel (Ayre & Scally, 2014; Lawshe, 1975) where to agree that an indicator is essential CVR should exceed 0.636.

Results

The corpus consists of 16 indicators related to the USR measurement. They reached above the critical value required for 9 experts' panel which is 0.636 (Ayre & Scally, 2014), so these are essential indicators (Table 3.3). The content validity of each indicator resulted in the omission of two dimensions—economic and ethical. Nevertheless, the 10 indicators with the lower critical value than 0.636 (e.g., Public availability of the annual financial report; How do you communicate about corrective measures taken after detecting ethics breaches?) might be included if needed on a case-by-case basis, or at least each university could design organisation-specific indicators that correspond to its authenticity (e.g. mission, moral character).

Table 3.3   Essential indicators of USR measurement

Dimensions, items, and related indicators		CVR	Weight
Organisational			
Social commitment (e.g. volunteering; social networking)	How do you ensure the local visibility of your academic personnel?	0.78	0.25
Communication of university social responsibility	How does your university communicate institutional values and institutional positioning to internal stakeholders?	1	0.25
	How does your university communicate institutional values and institutional positioning to external stakeholders?	1	0.25
	What is communicated under university social responsibility?	0.78	0.25
Environmental			
Waste management	What waste do you recycle?	0.78	0.17
	Percentage of recycled paper in comparison with the total waste (per year)	0.78	0.17
	Percentage of recycled electronic device and batteries in comparison with the total waste (per year)	0.78	0.17
Responsible consumption	What alternative (change to: renewable) energy resources and device does your institution use?	0.78	0.17
	How does your university encourage use of recycled paper?	0.78	0.17
Purchases and acquisitions related to fair trade, environmental security	What eco-criteria for purchasing and acquiring goods and/or services do you envisage?	0.78	0.17
Educational			
Networking	What international accreditations are awarded to your university?	1	1
Social			
Support for disadvantaged social groups	Does your university ensure access of the study programme contents and venues to disabled people? If so, how?	0.78	0.20

(continued)

Table 3.3   (continued)

Dimensions, items, and related indicators		CVR	Weight
Academic activism	Do your students take part in university social projects?	1	0.20
	Describe in which university social projects your students are involved.	1	0.20
	Do your academic personnel take part in university social projects?	0.78	0.20
	Describe in which university social projects your personnel is involved.	0.78	0.20

LIMITATIONS

We offer this integrative framework of USR as an arena to improve university performance by involving its stakeholders in such a way that its outputs and outcomes would generate more apparent effects, so as to evidence the co-creation of more tangible social value. However, we should admit that we succeeded in capturing only immediate effects; therefore, orientation towards long-term impacts remains unchallenged.

The suggested indicators are sensitive and specific as is required from a rigid measure; however, reliability and feasibility of indicators was not estimated, as further comprehensive empirical research should be carried out. For example, a qualitative indicator "Does your university ensure access of the study programme contents and venues to disabled people? If so, how?" under the USR social dimension could be refined to address current global and all-time changing expectations and pressure from the RRI community (e.g. communicating research findings in open access papers and journals). Similarly, a qualitative indicator "What waste do you recycle?" under the USR environmental dimension could be revised to include such types of waste as printer toner, food from canteens and so on. These and other indicators (Table 3.3) should be treated just as an incipient development of robust measurement of USR which must be validated in other socio-cultural contexts as well.

DISCUSSION

The suggested set of indicators for a framework of the USR measurement as a multidimensional concept and multifaceted phenomenon is a starting point of discussions about what universities strive for and why they exist in an era of constant transformation. We attempted to develop an integrative framework in response to this question, to facilitate universities recalling their institutional values and rethinking their role in university governance and management while giving evidence on their socially responsible practices. Nevertheless, the suggested set of indicators for measuring USR should be considered as a social act for further USR contextualisation (e.g. using co-creation to deal with overarching organisational culture), but not as a determined and complete standard that indicates compliance-related practices. Hence, the suggested indicators, in contrast to prior attempts to capture USR indicators (Aristimuño, 2012; Esfijani & Chang, 2012; Moneva Abadía & Vallespín, 2012; Vallaeys et al., 2009), are sensitive, specific, but they should still be made reliable and feasible, and an agreement on units of qualitative and quantitative measurement should be achieved. Therefore, our study calls for further empirical research testing the integrative framework in a comparative perspective in different institutional and socio-cultural contexts. As a minimal attempt, the sample of experts could be enlarged to include international experts of CSR.

Furthermore, as Timmermans and Epstein (2010) assert, the creation of the standard demands the involvement of multiple university stakeholders and should respond to many other patterns. Therefore, our framework for measuring USR might vary due to the specificity of a university (e.g. its institutional values, organisational culture, and strategy), its scope, flexibility and other aspects, but as Soh (2014) states, any discrepancy should be avoided to remain adequate and well-guided. This could help to impart value for university-specific rules and practices and respect the uniqueness of a university. It is also essential to take into consideration that studies used to develop an integrative framework of USR echo the past; therefore, they lack a visionary perspective related to current and future needs.

Overall, our chapter lends support to the idea that seeing an integrative framework of USR as a standard may be pernicious. Sauder and Espeland (2009) provide many arguments as to how academic rankings impel institutional pressures and imitation of success and induce decontextualisation of university, deprive universities of the initial mission and discourage innovation. O'Sullivan (2016) specifies it as academic barbarism. Hence, instead of focusing on necessary institutional changes, universities concentrate their efforts on being evaluated as highly as possible, disregarding implicit forms of discrimination and long-term impact on society, which may be the case with, e.g., gender equality plans. That is to say that the integrative framework of USR suggested by us should serve foremost for making institutional changes in order to have social impact using certain authenticity-driven items but not focusing on the number of ticks in respective boxes, which often happens when organisations take a compliance-based approach.

CONCLUSIONS

In this chapter we aimed to develop a conceptually consolidated framework of USR as an integrative measurement tool for advancing the concept of institutional social responsibility and specifically concentrating on educational institutions, i.e. universities. In addition, we aimed to propose a set of qualitative indicators which could contribute to the continual improvement of university activities, taking a stakeholder perspective. We concluded with a set of eight items with 16 indicators covering organisational, social, environmental, and educational dimensions of USR, which we integrated from prior studies with an attempt to make a framework simple but not simplistic. Therefore, the suggested indicators, in contrast to prior studies, serve as guidelines for further authentic development.

The research implication of our study is four dimensions which we integrate into the concept of USR. However, as the framework lacks reliability, we suggest further validating the integrative framework of USR with international experts to increase the reliability of the suggested measurement tool, better understand different institutional missions and country-specific contexts and justify the generalisation of the framework of USR measurement to a more diverse academic community. The latter could serve as the basis to create a developmental scale based on the maturity of social responsibility. Examples of such a scale might be either core motives for social responsibility engagement (such as strategy-driven, stakeholder-driven, and values-driven; further see Groza et al., 2011), levels of integrating social responsibility in real life of universities (such as born CSR oriented, patching, thickening, positioning, relabelling, trimming and cooperating, further see Yuan, Bao, & Verbeke, 2011; such as minimum legal compliance, enlightened self-interest and proactive change, further see Stahl & Grigsby, 1997).

Additionally, we suggest refining the integrative framework of USR that can be achieved when empirical data are collected. This would allow to consolidate USR measurement, particularly bearing in mind that due to the globalisation of higher education and research universities would further seek for not only rethinking their governance model, but also making impact on a local community at the least. Moreover, the consolidation of USR measurement better elucidates a multi-dimensional perspective and improves definitions of these dimensions, their items and different character of indicators.

References

Adams, C. A. (2013). Sustainability reporting and performance management in universities. *Sustainability Accounting, Management and Policy Journal, 4*(3), 384–392.

Albert, S., & Whetten, D. (1985). Organizational identity. In L. L. Cummings & B. M. Staw (Eds.), *Research in organizational behaviour 7* (pp. 263–295). Greenwich, CT: JAI Press.

Aristimuño, M. (2012). La Valoración de la Responsabilidad Social Universitaria: Dimensiones e indicadores para su abordaje. *Copérnico, VIII*(16), 23–29.

Ayala-Rodríguez, N., Barreto, I., Rozas Ossandón, G., Castro, A., & Moreno, S. (2019). Social transcultural representations about the concept of university social responsibility. *Studies in Higher Education, 44*(2), 245–259.

Ayre, C., & Scally, A. J. (2014). Critical values for Lawshe's content validity ratio. *Measurement and Evaluation in Counseling and Development, 47*(1), 79–86.

Baur, D., & Schmitz, H. P. (2013). Corporations and NGOs: When accountability leads to co-optation. *Journal of Business Ethics, 106,* 9–21.

Borden, V., Coates, H., & Bringle, R. (2018). Emerging perspectives on measuring and classifying institutional performance. In E. Hazelkorn, H. Coates, & A. C. McCormick (Eds.), *Research handbook on quality, performance and accountability in higher education* (pp. 189–205). Cheltenham: Edward Palgrave Publishing.

Brundlandt, G. H. (1987). *Report of the world commission on environment and development: Our common future*. World Commission on Environment and Development. http://www.un-documents.net/our-common-future.pdf. Accessed 25 September 2020.

Burke, L., & Logsdon, J. M. (1996). How corporate social responsibility pays off. *Long Range Planning, 29*(4), 495–502.

Canelón, A. R. (2013). Responsabilidad Social Universitaria 2.0. Análisis de las páginas web de universidades de AUSJAL. *Revista internacional de relaciones públicas, 5*(III), 27–48.

Carroll, A. B. (1979). A three-dimensional conceptual model of corporate performance. *Academy of Management Review, 4,* 497–505.

Carroll, A. B. (1999). Corporate social responsibility—Evolution of a definitional construction. *Business and Society, 38*(3), 268–295.

De Boer, H. F., Enders, J., & Leisyte, L. (2007). Public sector reform in Dutch higher education: The organizational transformation of the university. *Public Administration, 85*(1), 27–46.

De Jong, M. D. T., & Van der Meer, M. (2017). How does it fit? Exploring the congruence between organizations and their corporate social responsibility (CSR) activities. *Journal of Business Ethics, 143,* 71–83.

Denzin, N. K. (1970). *The research act in sociology.* Chicago: Aldine.

Drori, G. S., Delmestri, G., & Oberg, A. (2016). The iconography of universities as institutional Narratives. *Higher Education, 71,* 163–180.

European Commission. (2011). *A renewed EU strategy 2011–14 for corporate social responsibility.* Communication from the Commission to the European Parliament, the Council, the European Economic and Social Committee and the Committee of the Regions. Brussels, 25 October 2011. COM(2011) 681 final. http://www.europarl.europa.eu/meetdocs/2009_2014/docume nts/com/com_com(2011)0681_/com_com(2011)0681_en.pdf. Accessed 25 September 2020.

Esfijani, A., & Chang, E. (2012). A fuzzy logic based approach for measuring virtual university social responsibility. In *Proceedings of the 2nd World conference on soft computing* (pp. 149–154).

Fray, A. M. (2007). Ethical behaviour and social responsibility in organizations: Process and evaluation. *Management Decision, 45*(1), 76–88.

Fuller, S. (2005). What makes universities unique? Updating the ideal for an entrepreneurial age. *Higher Education Management and Policy, 17*(3), 17–42.

García-Marzá, D. (2005). Trust and dialogue: Theoretical approaches to ethics auditing. *Journal of Business Ethics, 57,* 209–219.

Gburi, I. (2015). The university and market value(s). *Our Schools/Our Selves, 25*(1), 149–157.

Godínez Valdés, B. A., Santos, R. C., & Hernández, N. J. (2014). Indicadores de responsabilidad social universitaria desde la enseñanza del postgrado en Ciencia, Tecnologia y Sociedad. In *Conferencia Científica Internacional "Ucencia 2014",* 24–26 April, Ecuador (pp. 1–12).

Gómez, L., Pujols, A., Alvarado, Y., & Vargas, L. (2018). Social responsibility in higher educational institutions: An exploratory study. In D. Crowther, S. Seifi, A. Moyeen (Eds.), *The goals of sustainable development: Approaches to global sustainability, markets, and governance* (pp. 215–230). Singapore: Springer.

Groza, M. D., Pronschinske, M. R., & Walker, M. (2011). Perceived organizational motives and consumer responses to proactive and reactive CSR. *Journal of Business Ethics, 102*(4), 639–652.

Henkel, M. (1997). Academic values and the university as corporate enterprise. *Higher Education Quarterly, 51*(2), 134–143.

Herrera, M. E., & Sánchez, Y. (2017). La responsabilidad social universitaria: un enfoque desde los diplomados del decanato de ciencias económicas y empresariales de la Universidad Centroccidental Lisandro Alvarado. *Gestión y Gerencia, 11*(1), 1–25.

Huhtala, M., Kangas, M., Kaptein, M., & Feldt, T. (2018). The shortened corporate ethical virtues scale: Measurement invariance and mean differences across two occupational groups. *Business Ethics: A European Review, 27*(3), 238–247.

Jongbloed, B., Enders, J., & Salerno, C. (2008). Higher education and its communities: Interconnections, interdependencies and a research agenda. *Higher Education, 56*(3), 303–324.

Kaptein, M. (2008). Developing and testing a measure for the ethical culture of organizations: The corporate ethics virtue model. *Journal of Organisational Behaviour, 29*, 923–947.

Kaptein, M. (2011). From inaction to external whistleblowing: The influence of the ethical culture of organizations on employee responses to observed wrongdoing. *Journal of Business Ethics, 98*, 513–530.

Krizek, K. J., Newport, D., White, J., & Townsend, A. R. (2012). Higher education's sustainability imperative: How to practically respond? *International Journal of Sustainability in Higher Education, 13*(1), 19–33.

Lawshe, C. H. (1975). A quantitative approach to content validity. *Personnel Psychology, 28*(4), 563–575.

Leja, K. (2010). A socially responsible university—An attempt to approach the system. *Contemporary Management Quarterly, 2–3*, 21–33.

Mainz, J. (2003). Defining and classifying clinical indicators for quality improvement. *International Journal for Quality in Health Care, 15*(6), 523–530.

McDonald, G. M. (2009). An anthology of codes of ethics. *European Business Review, 21*(4), 344–372.

McNay, I. (2007). Values, principles and integrity: Academic and professional standards in UK higher education. *Higher Education Management and Policy, 19*(3), 1–24.

Meyer, J. W., Ramirez, F. O., Frank, D. J., & Schofer, E. (2007). Higher education as an institution. In P. Gumport (Ed.), *The sociology of higher education: Contributions and their contexts* (pp. 25–49). Maryland: Johns Hopkins University.

Moneva Abadía, J. M. M., & Vallespín, E. M. (2012). Universidad y desarrollo sostenible: análisis de la rendición de cuentas de las universidades públicas desde un enfoque de responsabilidad social. *RIGC, X*(19), 1–18.

Noguera, J. J. M., Moncayo, J. E., & Martí-Vilar, M. (2014). Revisión de propuestas metodológicas para evaluar la responsabilidad social universitaria. *Revista Digital de Investigación en Docencia Universitaria, 8*(1), 77–94.

O'Sullivan, M. (2016). *Academic barbarism, universities and inequality.* Hampshire: Palgrave Macmillan.

Palinkas, L. A., Horwitz, S. M., Green, C. A., Wisdom, J. P., Duan, N., & Hoagwood, K. (2015). Purposeful sampling for qualitative data collection and analysis in mixed method implementation research. *Administration and Policy in Mental Health, 42*(5), 533–544.

Patton, M. Q. (2002). *Qualitative research and evaluation methods* (3rd ed.). Thousand Oaks: Sage.

Păunescu, C., Drăgan (Gilmeanu), D., & Găucă, O. (2017). Examining obligations to society for QS Stars best ranked universities in social responsibility. *Management & Marketing: Challenges for the Knowledge Society, 12*(4), 551–570.

Polese, F., & Monetta, G. (2006). Value creation and related measurement in universities: An empirical application. *Total Quality Management, 17*(2), 243–263.

Pollitt, C., & Bouckaert, G. (2000). *Public management reform: An international comparison.* Oxford: Oxford University Press.

Pučėtaitė, R., Novelskaitė, A., Lämsä, A.-M., & Riivari, E. (2016). The relationship between ethical organisational culture and organisational innovativeness: Comparison of findings from Finland and Lithuania. *Journal of Business Ethics, 139*(4), 685–700.

Rinne, R., & Koivula, J. (2005). The changing place of the university and a clash of values: The entrepreneurial university in the European knowledge society a review of the literature. *Higher Education Management and Policy, 17*(3), 91–123.

Rodríguez, N. A., & Hernández, B. (2017). Responsabilidad social universitaria un actor ignorado: el personal no docente. *Eureka, 14*(2), 240–254.

Rosenzweig, R. M. (1999–2000). Universities change, core values should not. *Issues in Science & Technology, 16*(2), 59–64.

Rubin, H. R., Pronovost, P., & Diette, G. B. (2001). From a process of care to a measure: The development and testing of a quality indicator. *International Journal for Quality in Health Care, 13*(6), 489–496.

Sauder, M., & Espeland, W. N. (2009). The discipline of rankings: Tight coupling and organizational change. *American Sociological Review, 74,* 63–82.

Sheehy, B. (2015). Defining CSR: Problems and solutions. *Journal of Business Ethics, 131,* 625–648.

Soh, K. (2014). Nominal versus attained weights in Universitas 21 Ranking. *Studies in Higher Education, 39*(6), 944–951.

Stadler, A., Andrade dos Reis, E., Arantes, E. C., & Del Corso, J. M. (2017). Study on professors' perception with respect to higher education institutions' socially responsible initiatives. *Brazilian Business Review, 14*(6), 592–608.

Stahl, M. J., & Grigsby, D. W. (1997). *Strategic management: Total quality & global competition*. Oxford: Blackwell.

Tauginienė, L., & Urbanovič, J. (2018). Social responsibility in transition of stakeholders—From the school to the university. In S. Seifi & D. Crowther (Eds.), *Stakeholders: Governance and responsibility, developments in corporate governance and responsibility* (Vol. 14, pp. 143–163). Bingley: Emerald Group Publishing.

The evolution of Responsible Research and Innovation in Europe: The MoRRI indicators report (D4.3). MoRRI consortium, February 2018. https://morri.net lify.com/reports/2018-02-21-the-evolution-of-responsible-research-and-inn ovation-in-europe-the-morri-indicators-report-d4-3. Accessed 25 September 2020.

Thomas, B., & Lucas, K. (2019). Development and validation of the workplace dignity scale. *Group and Organization Management, 44*(1), 72–111.

Timmermans, S., & Epstein, S. (2010). A world of standards but not a standard world: Toward a sociology of standards and standartization. *Annual Review of Sociology, 36,* 69–89.

Turker, D. (2018a). Socially responsible finance and accounting. In D. Turker (Ed.), *Managing social responsibility: Functional strategies, decisions and practices* (pp. 115–130). Cham: Springer International Publishing AG part of Springer Nature.

Turker, D. (2018b). Strategy and Social Responsibility. In D. Turker (Ed.), *Managing Social Responsibility: Functional strategies, decisions and practices* (pp. 43–58). Cham: Springer International Publishing AG part of Springer Nature.

Vallaeys, F. (2013). University Social Responsibility: A mature and responsible definition. In C. Escrigas, J. G. Sánchez, B. L. Hall, R. Tandon (Eds.), *Higher education in the world 5: Knowledge, engagement & higher education: Contributing to social change* (pp. 88–96). Global University Network for Innovation.

Vallaeys, F., De la Cruz, C., & Sasia, P. (2009). *Responsabilidad Social Universitaria, Manual de Primeros Pasos*. México: McGraw-Hill Interamericana Editores and Banco Interamericano de Desarrollo.

Viteri-Moya, J., Jácome-Villacres, M. B. J., & Medina-León, C. A. (2013). Modelo conceptual para la planificación estratégica con la incorporación de la responsabilidad social universitaria. *Ingeniería Industrial, XXXIV*(1), 77–86.

Wan-Jan, W. S. (2006). Defining corporate social responsibility. *Journal of Public Affairs, 6,* 176–184.

Wieland, J. (2001). The ethics of governance. *Business Ethics Quarterly, 11*(1), 73–87.

Wigmore-Álvarez, A., & Ruiz-Lozano, M. (2014). The United Nations global compact progress reports as management control instruments for social responsibility at Spanish Universities. *SAGE Open, 4*(2), 1–12.

Winter, R. P., & O'Donohue, W. (2012). Academic identity tensions in the public university: Which values really matter? *Journal of Higher Education Policy and Management, 34*(6), 565–573.

Young, S., Nagpal, S., & Adams, C. A. (2016). Sustainable procurement in Australian and UK universities. *Public Management Review, 16*(7), 993–1016.

Yuan, W., Bao, Y., & Verbeke, A. (2011). Integrating CST initiatives in business: An organizing framework. *Journal of Business Ethics, 101*(75), 75–92.

CHAPTER 4

Evaluating University Social Contribution: Insights and Concepts from Chinese Higher Education

Xi Hong, Lu Liu, Sara Bice, and Hamish Coates

MAKING PERSPECTIVES AND PLATFORMS FOR VALUE

At the start of April 2020, President Qiu Yong of Tsinghua University wrote in a global higher education newspaper that it was "Time for universities to show their commitment to society" (Qiu, 2020). "As COVID-19 continues to spread around the world", he argued, [it] "reminds us that we share a global community" and that "Great universities should proactively respond to the challenges and shoulder their

X. Hong · H. Coates
Tsinghua University, Beijing, China
e-mail: hongx18@mails.tsinghua.edu.cn

L. Liu
Jiangsu University, Zhenjiang, China

S. Bice
The Australian National University, Canberra, ACT, Australia
e-mail: Sara.Bice@anu.edu.au

© The Author(s), under exclusive license to Springer Nature   49
Switzerland AG 2021
L. Tauginienė and R. Pučėtaitė (eds.), *Managing Social Responsibility in Universities*, https://doi.org/10.1007/978-3-030-70013-3_4

responsibilities at such times to demonstrate their commitment to society". Universities are, he asserted, "The lighthouse of human civilisation" (Qiu, 2020).

These are remarkable statements which prescribe new directions for higher education, particularly as they come from one of the top universities in China, the country which has led the twenty-first century charge on bibliometrics. First, they make clear the vitality and significance of universities, and the capacity of these resilient institutions to tackle and solve huge and complex problems. Such observation charges straight through the declining trust in and commitment towards universities displayed in many major higher education systems in recent decades. Universities have a renewed 'social license to operate' (Bice, Poole, & Sullivan, 2017) which is central and thriving future in building future global affairs. Second, particularly as they come from the top of Chinese higher education, the statements convey that universities must not shirk from embracing large and complex challenges, and instead must work with governments and civil society to ensure productive advance. This means tackling large issues around sustainability, peace, education, and health. It signals a major reorientation away from focusing on the production of rankings-relevant scientific articles. Third, the statements signal that universities, as large and influential institutions, must become responsive to society. Universities are part of the communities which surround and sustain them, including local areas, professions, global science, and strategic interests. Fourth, and most pointedly for this chapter, universities must find ways to show or prove that they are excellent at partnering with society. This creates the need for indicators, data, and reports.

Research on the social engagement of universities remains in its infancy, though it has grown more popular, propelled by the quest for new relevance in the post-COVID-19 world. As a recent cross-national scan has revealed (Liu, Hong, Li, & Coates, 2020), this is an eclectic field and it is helpful to signpost areas being developed. There is increasing interest regarding 'university sustainability'. Such research touches on the 'campus', on the emergence of cross-disciplinary fields, and on the emergence of new forms of practice (Eaton, Hugher, & MacGregor, 2016; Leal Filho & Bardi, 2019; Leal Filho et al., 2019; Peterson & Wood, 2016). Research also focuses on various formal forms of 'reporting'. Such reporting has been spurred by broad global interest in the topic, and within higher education by the Talloires Declaration (Corcoran & Wals, 2004), the formation of organisations like the Association for the Advancement of Sustainability in Higher Education (AASHE) and renewed focus by government agencies, such as the Higher Education Funding Council for England (HEFCE, 2014). In 2014, for example, about 100 universities world-wide employed the AASHE Sustainability Tracking, Assessment and Ranking System (STARS) (STARS, 2014). Amaral, Martins, and Gouveia (2015) enumerate several university-specific sustainability reporting frameworks in a compelling review of sustainability in higher education. These include STARS, the Sustainability Tool for Auditing Curricula in Higher Education (STAUNCH) and Lozano's (2011) Graphical Assessment of Sustainability in Universities (GASU), among others. One further stream of research focuses on 'social contribution' more broadly. Topics in this area range across the work roles of faculty and 'third-stream professionals', university-business collaborations, and research impact evaluations. As the higher education sector moves more squarely into public life, questions about global and public governance are also playing a part (e.g. Dollinger, Coates, Bexley, Croucher, & Naylor, 2018; Grant, 2015; Macfarlane, 2011). These areas of inquiry naturally broaden discussion beyond universities into wider socioeconomic worlds.

It is useful, therefore, to find ways of making sense of this large, eclectic, and especially important field. Fitting phenomena within existing sociological theories and frameworks is one means of doing this. Another option, which is touched on in the next section, is to descriptively appraise salient policies and practices. Another option, adopted in this paper, is to invoke methodologies and epistemologies from the field of education evaluation and design (Coates, 2020) to create models and indicators which help understand hence progress university social engagement and contribution. This chapter advances in this direction, building on recent large-scale policy innovation undertaken in China, which is designed to have broader international relevance. This research was conducted with the broad interest of helping to guide the future role of universities in society. As higher education shifts into new futures one large-scale concern narrows around how to understand hence boost the 'value' created and contributed to a diverse range of communities. What ideas, stories, forms of evaluation, information and data can shape transformation and growth? Of course, many institutions and systems are fuelled by broader mandates like nation-building, scientific advance, and community development, but these big ideas still must be distilled into specific platforms, indicators, and instruments.

These future platforms, indicators and instruments need to differ in significant ways to those designed in the past and still in widespread use today. The details are tilled below, but the crux goes to the need not just for growth or performance or quality but above all else for distinctive forms of value. Value in this context reflects the need to create, discover and contribute more than is consumed. The concept of 'net zero' has popularised this ethos with respect to emissions economies, but the core idea can be expanded well beyond environmental concerns and pushed further into the territory of 'net positive'. Net positive, in short, is about putting back more than is taken out. For universities, there must be proof that the admission, education, and graduation of students returns more value than it consumes. Research must discover, create, and make more value than goes into it. Institutions and the people who swirl through them must parlay resources received into more substantial social, environmental, and economical contributions. Universities should create more and different communities than they are initially asked to serve.

Higher education needs to move a long way to touch, embrace and progress in net positive ways. First, it is necessary to unshackle from current operating environments which have come to threaten system and institutional growth. This is because environmental mechanisms built up over the last few decades are yielding diminishing returns. It is time to open space and options for creative development, imagining different futures. Doing this makes it possible to define perspectives helpful for paving alternative value indicators. Tracing implications of these activities is helpful for spurring entrepreneurial transformations.

To move in this direction, therefore, this chapter examines the development of social contribution indicators in Chinese higher education. After launching the analysis, the chapter examines how social engagement contributions are being reframed in Chinese higher education. The discussion moves to looking at the curation of recent policy research which has sought to design novel information which has the potential to illuminate and guide growth. The final section evaluates progress so far, and options for further development. The chapter synthesizes theoretical perspectives, contributes an evaluation framework, and articulates contemporary circumstances in the world's largest higher education system.

Reframing Social Responsibilities

As signalled by the idea of being net positive, major thinking and developing is taking place around sustainability and social impact indicators. Indeed, there are ample signs that as these new axiological conceptualisations unfold the social dimension is playing not just a compartmentalized functional role as one university 'vertical' among others, but that its relevance and influence is much broader. As Fig. 4.1 conveys, this field of work appears to have moved from being 'beyond' or 'outside' academic work and ignored or dismissed (remote phase), to being the 'recipient' of university work (negotiated phase), to being the shaper and co-creator as well as recipient of all academic and institutional functions (integrated phase). This is a general evolutionary observation, of course, which varies according to context, though the general framework does help make sense of different particularities.

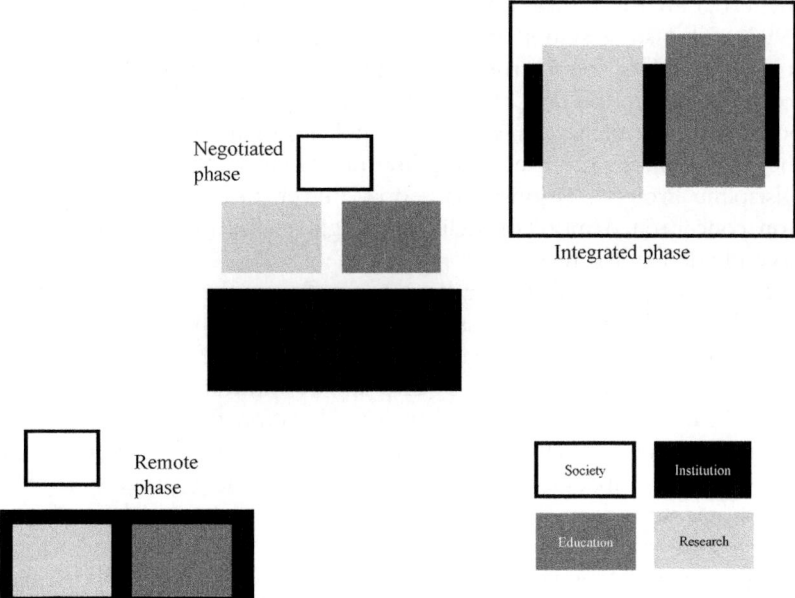

Fig. 4.1 Repositioning significance of social dimensions

This evolution can be observed and exemplified in three distinct developmental periods of Chinese higher education which have been shaped by national policies and social issues. In the early period after the establishment of the People's Republic of China, universities focused mainly on talent training. There was a remote relationship between universities and society. This situation changed after opening-up in the late 1970s, which emphasized socialist modernization and economic development as core to national construction. This elevated the role of scientific discovery and social service. This period laid the initial keystone of Chinese universities' social service function, which was tied closely to technical and economic fields, such as research and technology achievement conversion and economic consultation.

The next period was signified by a major program to modernize Chinese universities which began in the 1990s. This focused on research in technological fields, and also on the training of outstanding scholars and professionals for key fields. In 1993, China's State Council enacted the Program for Education Reform and Development (State Council, 1993). This suggested that higher education should strive to develop specialized education for rural areas, small and medium-sized enterprises, township enterprises and the tertiary industry, and expand the scale of postgraduate students. This era led to policies such as the '211 Project', the '985 Project', the 'Key Discipline Innovation Platform' and the 'Key Discipline Project'. During this period, universities' social service function concentrated more on delivering high-quality human resources to urgently demanded fields.

Several major reforms have been enacted over the last decade. Most broadly, social engagement has been emphasized by the Chinese government and its intermediary organs through programs of quality evaluation. For instance, the Audit of Undergraduate Education and Teaching (AUET) conducted by the Ministry of Education from 2014 to 2018, mainly evaluated undergraduate education in terms of orientation and goals, faculty capability, teaching resources, training process, student development, and quality assurance. But it also advocated the exchange of teaching resources and cooperation between universities and society (MOE, 2013). Organized by the China Academic Degrees and Graduate Education Development Centre (CDGDC), the China University Subject Rankings (CUSR) evaluated graduate courses in terms of "social service and subject reputation" (CDGDC, 2018). It required institutions to submit the overall situation and representative cases of their contribution in serving economic and social construction. The evaluations have been conducted by experts along with practitioners from industry, enterprise, and international agencies.

A much more pointed emphasis has been placed on social matters since the launch of the 'double world class' (DWC) suite of reforms. In 2015, China's Central Party Committee and the State Council of China announced plans for the coordination and promotion of world-class universities and first-class discipline building (State Council, 2015). This double-world class strategy has sought to further strengthen China's competitiveness in education and research while laying foundations for long-term development, but also raising the level of social service and engagement between higher education institutions and local communities. In 2017, a list of 42 universities and 95 disciplines was released. One of the key selection standards is contribution in social service, including industry-university-institute cooperation, cooperative talent training, conversion of research achievements, and leading national economic, industrial, and technological upgrading (MOE, 2017a). In 2018, the government issued the Notice on Guiding Opinions on Speeding up the Construction of Double-World-Class Universities, which especially stimulated selected universities to strengthen social service by, for instance, serving regional and national key strategies, promoting traditional culture, and deepening international cooperation (MOE, 2018). In this period, universities' social service functions have achieved a more independent status, which is not only regarded as the extension of scientific research and talent training, but has also included more dimensions such as improving public scientific and humanistic quality, carrying forward and developing outstanding traditional culture, providing decision-making consultation for government and other social organizations, leading the international communication and cooperation (MOE, 2010). The relationship between universities' and society has been framed as win/win cooperation, with universities playing active roles in leading social innovation, ventures, and reform. The participants in this process have expanded to broader members, such as faculty, staff, and students, as well as broader governmental and civil institutions.

Combined, as noted at the outset with respect to the President Qiu Yong's statements, these ideas point to a shift in the logic guiding higher education. Rather than parlay tuition revenue into research and specifically publication outcomes to inflate the university brand to stimulate consumption and growth, labelled as "world-class logic" (Salmi,

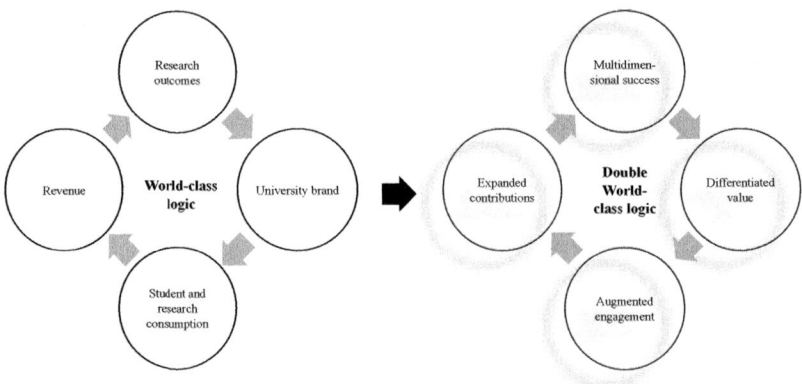

Fig. 4.2 Creating new higher education value

2009) in Fig. 4.2, emphasis shifts to a new 'double world class logic' in which universities create value on many fronts, parlay this into many forms of augmented engagement, expand their scope and scale of their contributions, and generate multidimensional successes.

CURATING NEW PERSPECTIVES

This conceptual and evolutionary framing outlines the growing role of Chinese universities with regards to social contribution. As part of governmental and institutional development new value indicators are required to push university performance in net positive directions. What sort of information is likely to impel future higher education leaders to reach outside national policy systems and create distinctive forms of value? This is a complex matter, as a review by Borden and Holthaus (2018) conveys. There remains a pressing need for information that helps institutions and people discover how to best engage, create, and contribute with higher education. Such information must focus on university outcomes and processes as much as inputs like funding and admissions. Echoing shifts underway in other sectors, it must give insight into impact and value. As well, information must focus on individuals as well as institutions and systems. It must go beyond university research activities to consider other core facets of academic work, notably education, but also broader socioeconomic forms of engagement. The information must be dynamically shaped by clever algorithms rather than presented as static ordinal lists.

In building out such work several perspectives are important to keep in mind. For instance, any system-level evaluation architecture such as this should be framed by appropriate governance (Austin & Jones, 2015). Key governance theories examine different agencies, responsibility configurations, and interactions. They unpack theories of governance/policy structures, which articulate the espoused and actual ways in which higher education operates. They prise open theories of institutional diversity, which focus on how to maximise value/productivity and relevance of higher education institutions to the broader community. Such thinking must frame the formation of novel information regarding university social contribution and responsibility.

As well, the value and impact of evaluation information is lost unless it resonates with and compels university leaders to improve. To be effective new perspectives on social contribution should rest on theories of higher education leadership. Contemporary university leaders must marry competing academic (education and research) with external (commercial and political) imperatives. In building new insights, it is important to draw on management approaches that help explain how higher education institutions use information (Webber & Calderon, 2015). Unless indicators entice universities to step ahead, they fail to capture the imagination of leaders and spur management improvements.

Of course, real change in higher education hinges on transformation of faculty work. Faculty, not just university or policy leaders, must be inspired and engaged to change their performance. To enact change at this level any information must engage with general theories of academic work and reform, as well as functional insights into education, research, and engagement. Unlike the prevailing rankings, which have proved difficult to translate in interpretable ways by actual faculty, data on social engagement should be immediately useful to help people do better in their work. This frames the need for information on the contexts which shape core education and research work. Also, it creates the need for reports which engage and inspire faculty and academic managers.

Any disclosures about higher education must first and foremost be relevant to the public, particularly people who know little about universities, and particularly when it concerns how they can engage. As Coates (2017b) articulates, key insights on how to do this stem from the large body of work developed in recent decades on academic, institutional, and social choice. In particular, to that information on social contribution is relevant and sustainable it should take account of theories of consumer purchasing, emerging theories of social impact and co-creation and theories of higher education markets. This discourse must stretch people's interest beyond the promotion of luxury goods to instead create new forms of multidimensional and multilevel value for all universities.

Designing Information

Recent large-scale evaluation design has shown a way to build up the conceptual and institutional infrastructure required to advance these ideas. This work stemmed from the design of a multidimensional architecture for China's DWC strategy (Zhong, Liu, Coates, & Kuh, 2019). Drawing from research conducted between 2017 and 2020, this discussion details the optimal design of such an architecture, then the underpinning research perspectives.

The architecture was designed to spotlight four dimensions, namely education success, research productivity, social contribution, and institutional growth. The dimensions signposted in Fig. 4.3 flow from what decades of higher education and broader public policy research flag as important to develop. They embrace but also step beyond research and chart new conversations and innovations. These areas are framed to be of immediate relevance to the system policy, institutional leadership, academic practice, and consumer interests discussed above. They go well beyond institution-level preoccupations with research to provide insights into fields of interest to many people. Emphasising these areas is needed to shift into the integrated phase noted above.

Education is the core of most of the world's higher education institutions. The policy research affirmed that a useful architecture should embrace education success in terms of student engagement, learning outcomes and career development. It should draw from work which has reshaped how students, business, universities, and the public pursue education success. This work draws on investigations of student admissions, studies of student engagement, and studies of learning outcomes as people progress through higher education and studies of graduate destinations and career progression. Foundation work has been laid in these areas over the last decade, furnishing necessary data and technology. Such work has not yielded perfect solutions, but it is arguably far more

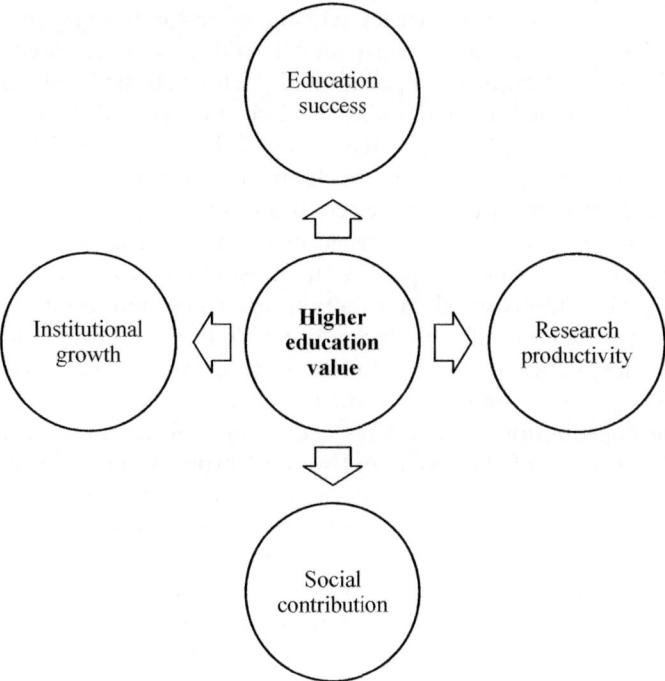

Fig. 4.3 Higher education value dimensions

advanced than was bibliometrics when it was parlayed into global rank-ings. As has been evident in the rise of bibliometric science over the last decade, resting system and institution growth expectations on indicators will ensure rapid technical development. Education is too important to ignore and let wane.

Research productivity comprises faculty output, research quality and academic impact. Accordingly, the design research affirmed that the archi-tecture should build on excellent prior work evaluating research and augment and advance this with emerging insights into new forms of research relevance and impact. To date, research rankings have exploited bibliometric data to emphasise the volume and peer-recognition of a researcher's or department's output. While ready to hand, these measures fail to say anything about the broader contribution of research (Grant, 2015). To frame future practice, it is essential to draw on or chart the need for more advanced metrics relating of research engagement and impact. These metrics cover conventional products derived directly from research like publications and patents and doctoral students, but also step beyond to examine links with industry, public impact, and the creation of shared value (Bice & Coates, 2016; Bice, Nealy, & Einfeld, 2019). New data on research has the capacity to stimulate new kinds of research.

Social contribution can be viewed as spanning regional engagement, national development, and international impact. The scope of such engagement is of course shaped by the mission and scale of the university. In general terms social contribution may be organized into forms of engagement that stem from education, research, or institution activities. For instance, education-related forms of engagement might include the extent of open courseware, the provision of community-based education, and the contribution of graduates and alumni. Research contributions can take account of the scope and scale of projects and start-ups, staff exchanges, engagement via media and lectures, and more traditional academic service contributions. Institution-related contributions might take account of a university's networks and partnerships, the public use of facilities, and even the provision of strategic plans and budgets for such engagement. To measure these facets of social influence, the architecture can be designed to integrate developments in corporate governance and social impact assessment to chart new ways for understanding and creating the social engagement of universities and disciplinary fields. This means touching on techniques related to organisational social responsibility, university-industry relations, and the links between fields and the industries and professions that they represent. Much of the technical and practical efforts required in this area involve bringing universities into broader alignment with the way other major sectors report their social influence.

Table 4.1 delves deeper with relation to the social contribution dimension, presenting a potential shortlist of feasible indicators. In this articulation, the social value of education is construed not just by the number of students admitted, retained, and graduated, but also by the sort of indicators listed in. The value of research is much more than publications and about the relevance and contribution. Institutional forms of engagement go to the way in which universities partner and embrace relevant communities. Spurred by the need for national and public relevance, this work is building fast in Asia. As noted at the outset of this chapter, this is a young

Table 4.1 Social contribution indicators

Educational contributions	Research contributions	Institutional contributions
Lifelong learning	*Social partnerships*	*Social infrastructure*
Public education	Staff exchanges	Public museums
Public library access	Start-ups and spin-offs	Campus public use
Online course provision	Academic community service	
Continuing education resources	Science and business parks	
Graduate contributions	*Public accessibility*	*Public engagement*
Graduate career services	Open publication	Community plans
Alumni contributions	Media contribution	Local tourism
Graduate regional contributions	Project accessibility	Networks and partnerships
		Public governance
		Sports engagement
		Community-based projects
Student engagement	*Integration and conversion*	
Summer school participation	Public lectures	
Student diversity	Public research governance	
Service-learning options	Patents and licenses	
Program industry alignment	Commercial revenue streams	

field and there is some way to go to build and deliver mature indicators. Development work will need to confront very divergent stakeholder perspectives, the blossoming of frameworks, the challenges of context, and the need for grounding in concrete institutional life.

Any important facet of any reporting system is that it helps higher education institutions themselves develop. Institution growth is about governance and leadership, management effectiveness, and the creation of distinctive value. Top-ranked 'world-class' universities comprise a tiny fraction of all institutions, about one per cent, yet all universities can and should be engaged to become excellent in their own distinctive ways. To encourage this, as conveyed by governance and leadership research, indicator systems must provide scope for each university to define and demonstrate their own unique excellence. To enable this, the indicator architecture should draw on proven and innovative managerial and actuarial perspectives on how to understand and advance the success/productivity of higher education institutions. Emerging policy-level research across ten countries in Asia has proven the feasibility of collecting and compiling such data (Coates, 2017a; Moore, Coates, & Croucher, 2019; Zhong, Coates, & Shi, 2019). It should define ways to reflect productivity that matter to all universities, and also ways which enable distinctive expressions aligned with each institution's strategy.

These four areas, at least, are both necessary in any robust set of dimensions. The dimensions cover what is conventionally identified as the primary academic functions. Each adds its own value and is appropriately general to cover relevant information needs. For instance, excellent research and education can go hand-in-hand, but they often do not, and any assumption that great research implies education success Dimension is easy to prove false (Gu, Lu, & Shi, 2007; Zhang & Guo, 2014). Likewise, being managed well does not necessitate that a university is socially influential. Ultimately, links between these four dimensions and relevant underpinning metrics are contingent and shaped by a range of contexts and interests. This implies the need for a dynamic reporting platform that enables end users to shape what they seek to discover. Continuing to rely on static and highly aggregated research metrics will not unlock the new value sought for future higher education.

If this broad dimensional architecture is accepted, then it paves the need and foundations for designing indicators which really define and establish the social characteristics of future university. This is a complex task, for everyone sees this matter as important, which has led to wild proliferation of frameworks, indicators, data suggestions, and reports. These frameworks furnish different perspectives, bring out the complexities of drawing tight boundaries around inherently complex academic work, reveal that much prior work has had gained little traction, and revealed the need to step beyond Anglo-European perspectives, or at least to identify social characteristics which are globally generalisable. There is a pressing need to advance major research in this field, not least which is relevant to Asia given estimates that two-thirds of higher education will be in this region by 2030 (OECD, 2016).

Building out this frontier requires distillation of a vast array of research and practice. A review of prior literature was conducted (e.g. Bice & Coates, 2016; BUSC, 2020; Clifford & Hazenberg, 2015; Garlick & Langworthy, 2008; Key, 1996; KPMG, 2020; Motahisa, 2009; Pan & Cui, 2016; NIAD-UE, 2014; Temple, Story, & Delaforce, 2005; Tokyo Tech, 2017). This review helped build a long list of potential indicators. Phenomenological techniques were used to collate these in ways relevant to prestigious Asian universities (Zhong, Coates, & Shi, 2019). Consultation with experts and stakeholders then helped to shortlist the most promising options.

Of course, sufficiently engaging platforms are needed to advance this new aperture. Rather than framing academic activities using functional terms like 'research', 'education', 'engagement' and 'administration', research has affirmed the importance of the cross-cutting ideas phrased above such as education success, research productivity, social influence and institution governance. Such headline terms might be distinguished into more granular ideas, which in turn can be underpinned by the substantial information that swirls around higher education. Software can then blend and slice this information in clever ways to suit myriad contexts and interests. To be effective, these platforms must empower people with intelligence on how they can create meaningful higher education experiences.

Moving into Practice

The intentions driving development in this area are clear. At the broadest level, enhancing engagement seeks to ensure that contemporary/future university governance, management and administration processes support effective social engagement. Progress in this area should ensure that university is accessible, outward reaching and responsive to its communities. It should increase the social, environmental, and economic value of research to university's communities. Aligning and situating academic programs with social contexts should help design and deliver high quality teaching, learning and research which responds to social needs. Designing indicators to collect data from multiple regions or multiple universities should inform monitoring, improvement, and enhancement.

These are admirable ideas but, as their very substance conveys, are wasted unless they help make universities more relevant to society. By way of conclusion, therefore, how then to evaluate the current state of play? What major trends can be seen across China, and what are the emerging avenues for development? It is difficult to build a comprehensive picture given the scale and rapid development of the country and higher education system, and given the lack of monitoring indicators, it is possible to draw out important informative observations.

Greater policy emphasis on social engagement has indeed spurred substantial activity and progress. In recent years, Chinese universities have been successful in translating and transferring research and technology into practical applications. In 2015, for instance, Chinese institutions received more than 35 billion yuan (about US$5 billion) of horizontal research funds, and two billion yuan (about US$300 million) trading scientific and technological achievements (MOE, 2017b). Among the 1,762 universities surveyed, 573 reported that they had established specialized institutions for the conversion of technological achievements. From 2006 to 2015, the number of technology conversion contracts signed by universities as sellers increased steadily, reaching 57,000 in 2015 (MOE, 2017b). Institutions have also contributed in social, cultural and international ways such as serving regional major strategic issues by providing consultation and solutions, promoting the development of poverty-stricken areas by donating equipment and providing special recruitment for students, guiding cultural inheritance by organizing public fora and seminars about traditional Chinese culture and establishing international joint research centres (MOE, 2009a, 2009b, 2017b, 2020).

Progress has also encountered challenges. First, the way in which universities are resourced still preferences what may be considered to be traditional scholarly or scientific endeavours. This, in turn, hinders the potential to contribute to promoting public well-being and lifelong learning. For example, many campuses remain gated, and most libraries and laboratories are not accessible to the public, except during special open days. Second, in spite of the progress in research and technology cooperation, there remain evident disconnects between the universities and industry. As Zhou, Tijssen, and Leydesdorff (2016) noted, Chinese universities are much less active in collaborations with local industry in terms of either publication productivity or collaboration intensity. The conversion rate of technological achievements has remained low for a long (Dollinger, Coates, Bexley, Croucher, & Naylor, 2018). The rate remained lower than five per cent in 2017 (Li & Coates, 2020). A persistent obstacle appears to involve helping universities engage effectively with local industry. Third, isomorphic striving for a homogenized perspective of status has hindered diversification and local engagement, as has been the case in most other major higher education contexts. Local universities, for instance, have sought to transform into comprehensive research universities, putting excessive emphasis on research activities. This has led to the neglect of various specific demands of regional communities in non-academic areas (Ni, 2014).

There remains ample scope for building new insights and information which have potential to enhance the engagement and contributions of universities with society. This analysis has articulated foundations for giving life to a new evaluation logic and architecture for higher education in which multidimensional and multilevel success drives new forms of diversified value, augment engagements, and expanded contributions. This work steps beyond limited institutional research-oriented lists to create engaging and sophisticated reports across a range of key areas. Packaged in engaging ways, these reports can spur new insights into higher education, enhancing sector activity and contribution. Research has defined the required structures, information, analyses, and reports (Coates, 2017b). It has revealed that progress requires collaboration among education researchers, university leaders, and software experts. It has revealed a particular need to build broader insights into social contribution, a core pillar which languishes in current rankings. It has affirmed the importance of linking institutional research, continuous quality improvement, and clarifying the value of higher education.

Of course, the real-world creation of innovation on this scale does not flow without obstacles. Self-evidently, the established international rankings are supported by power dynamics which underpin reputation and prestige. Many of the particularly prominent earlier generation reporting initiatives have also secured a first-mover advantage through being early entrants in a young field. The lack of courage and perceived need for reform is a hazard, particularly among powerful interests with stakes in the status quo, though the global tectonic forces sketched at the outset of this paper seem to be swinging with a forward momentum. Indicator definition and data collection has proved troublesome and costly, particularly in relation to education and engagement work. Establishing that data is robust on a large scale is always challenging, but there is substantial room to align techniques in this field with expected standards in school-level cross-national assessment studies. Clearly, development will be patterned by a range of forces.

References

Amaral, L. P., Martins, N., & Gouveia, J. B. (2015). Quest for a sustainable university: A review. *International Journal of Sustainability in Higher Education, 16*, 155–172.

Austin, I., & Jones, G. A. (2015). *Governance of higher education: Global perspectives, theories, and practices.* Abingdon: Routledge.

Bice, S., & Coates, H. (2016). University sustainability reporting: Taking stock of transparency. *Tertiary Education and Management, 22*(1), 1–18.

Bice, S., Nealy, K., & Einfeld, C. (2019). Next generation engagement: Setting a research agenda for community engagement in Australia's infrastructure sector. *Australian Journal of Public Administration, 78*(2), 290–310.

Bice, S., Poole, A., & Sullivan, H. (2017). *Public Policy in the Asian Century: Concepts, cases and futures.* Singapore: Springer.

Borden, V. M., & Holthaus, G. C. (2018). Accounting for student success: Academic and stakeholder perspectives that have shaped the discourse on student success in the United States. *International Journal of Chinese Education, 7*(1), 150–173.

Brown University Swearer Center (BUSC). (2020). *2020 Classification application information.* https://www.brown.edu/swearer/carnegie/2020-classification-application-information. Accessed 1 July 2020.

China Academic Degrees and Graduate Education Information (CDGDC). (2018). *Overview of the fourth round of China University subject rankings.* http://www.cdgdc.edu.cn/xwyyjsjyxx/xkpgjg/283494.shtml#1. Accessed 1 July 2020.

Clifford, J., & Hazenberg, R. (2015). Aligning the needs and requirements for social investment, commissioning for social value and effective social enterprises. E3M Policy Article.

Coates, H. (2017a). *Productivity in higher education: Research insights for universities and governments in Asia.* Tokyo: Asian Productivity Organisation.

Coates, H. (2017b). *The market for learning: Leading transparent higher education.* Dordrecht: Springer.

Coates, H. (2020). *Higher education design: Big deal partnerships, technologies and capabilities.* Singapore: Palgrave Macmillan.

Corcoran, P. B., & Wals, A. E. (2004). *Higher education and the challenge of sustainability.* Dordrecht: Kluwer Academic Publishers.

Dollinger, M., Coates, H., Bexley, E., Croucher, G., & Naylor, R. (2018). Framing international approaches to university-industry collaboration. *Policy Reviews in Higher Education, 2*(1), 105–127.

Eaton, M., Hugher, H. J., & MacGregor, J. (2016). *Contemplative approaches to sustainability in higher education.* Abingdon: Routledge.

Garlick, S., & Langworthy, A. (2008). Benchmarking university community engagement: Developing a national approach in Australia. *Higher Education Management and Policy: Higher Education and Regional Development, 20*(2), 153.

Grant, J. (2015). *The nature, scale and beneficiaries of research impact: An initial analysis of research excellence framework.* London: King's College London.

Gu, L., Lu, G., & Shi, B. (2007). An empirical study on the relation between college teaching and research. *Liaoning Educational Research, 3,* 25–27.

Higher Education Funding Council for England (HEFCE). (2014). *Sustainable development in higher education: HEFCE's role to date and a framework for its future actions.* Bristol: Higher Education Funding Council for England.

Key, S. (1996). Economics or education: The establishment of American land-grant universities. *The Journal of Higher Education, 67*(2), 196–220.

KPMG. (2020). *Carrots and sticks.* https://www.carrotsandsticks.net. Accessed 1 July 2020.

Leal Filho, W., & Bardi, U. (Eds.). (2019). *Sustainability on University Campuses: Learning, skills building and best practices.* Singapore: Springer.

Leal Filho, W., Salvia, A. L., Pretorius, R., Brandli, L., Manolas, E., Alves, F., et al. (Eds.). (2019). *Encyclopedia of sustainability in higher education.* Dordrecht: Springer.

Li, R., & Coates, H. (2020). Promoting social service of universities in Chinese context: International experience, practical issues and policy advices. *Journal of Higher Education Management, 14*(4), 96–106.

Liu, L., Hong, X., Li, R., & Coates, H. (2020). On the evaluation of university's contribution to society: The practice and enlightenment from America, Australia and Japan. *Tsinghua Journal of Education, 1,* 134–141.

Lozano, R. (2011). The state of sustainability reporting in universities. *International Journal of Sustainability in Higher Education, 12,* 67–78.

Macfarlane, B. (2011). The morphing of academic practice: Unbundling and the rise of the para-academic. *Higher Education Quarterly, 65*(1), 5–73.

Ministry of Education (MOE). (2009a). *East China Normal University enhances scientific research strength to serve regional economic and social development.* http://www.moe.gov.cn/jyb_xwfb/s6192/s133/s169/201004/t20 100419_84153.html. Accessed 1 July 2020.

Ministry of Education (MOE). (2009b). *The humanities and social sciences of Hunan University actively serve the economic and social construction.* http://

www.moe.gov.cn/jyb_xwfb/s6192/s133/s204/201004/t20100419_85004. html. Accessed 1 July 2020.

Ministry of Education (MOE). (2010). *Outline of the National Medium—And Long-Term Plan for Education Reform and Development (2010–2020)*. http://www.moe.gov.cn/srcsite/A01/s7048/201007/t20100729_171904. html. Accessed 1 July 2020.

Ministry of Education (MOE). (2013). *Scheme of the audit of undergraduate education and teaching in higher education institutions*. http://www.moe.gov. cn/srcsite/A08/s7056/201312/t20131212_160919.html. Accessed 1 July 2020.

Ministry of Education (MOE). (2017a). *Implementation measures to coordinate development of world-class universities and first-class disciplines construction (tentative)*. http://www.moe.gov.cn/srcsite/A22/moe_843/201701/ t20170125_295701.html. Accessed 1 July 2020.

Ministry of Education (MOE). (2017b). *Monitoring report on innovation capacity of Chinese Universities 2016 has been released*. http://www.moe. gov.cn/jyb_xwfb/s5147/201710/t20171010_315987.html. Accessed 1 July 2020.

Ministry of Education (MOE). (2018). *Notice on guiding opinions on speeding up the construction of double-world-class universities*. http://www.gov.cn/xin wen/2018-08/27/content_5316809.htm. Accessed 1 July 2020.

Ministry of Education (MOE). (2020). *South China Normal University accomplished a good job in attracting and training talents, and solidly promoting the construction of world-class disciplines*. http://www.moe.gov.cn/jyb_sjzl/ s3165/202003/t20200316_431658.html. Accessed 1 July 2020.

Moore, M., Coates, H., & Croucher, G. (2019). Measuring international higher education productivity: Lessons from nine countries in Asia. *Higher Education Forum, 16*, 69–84.

Motahisa, K. (2009). Incorporation of national universities in Japan design, implementation and consequences. *Asia Pacific Education Review, 10*(1), 59–67.

National Institution for Academic Degrees and University Evaluation (NIAD-UE). (2014). *Quality assurance system in higher education Japan*. http:// www.niad.ac.jp/english/overview_jp_e_ver2.pdf. Accessed 1 July 2020.

Ni, Z. (2014). Reflection on the social responsibility of universities based on the perspective of orientation and internal responsibility. *Education Review, 2*, 3–5.

Organisation for Economic Cooperation and Development (OECD). (2016). *Skills for a Digital World. 2016 Ministerial Meeting on the Digital Economy Background Report*. Paris: OECD.

Pan, L., & Cui, H. (2016). The new tendency of Carnegie classification of higher education institution in U.S.—Research of 2015 Carnegie elective community engagement classification. *International & Comparative Education, 7,* 79–84.

Peterson, R., & Wood, P. R. (2016). *Sustainability: Higher education's new fundamentalism.* Lakewood: Polaris Books.

Qiu, Y. (2020). *Time for universities to show their commitment to society.* https://www.universityworldnews.com/post.php?story=202004011548 15248. Accessed 1 July 2020.

Salmi, J. (2009). *The challenge of establishing world class universities.* The World Bank.

STARS. (2014). *STARS annual review 2014: Campus sustainability, ratings, innovations and best practice.* Colorado: AASHE.

State Council. (1993). *Program for education reform and development in China.* www.moe.gov.cn/jyb_sjzl/moe_177/tnull_2484.html. Accessed 1 July 2020.

State Council. (2015). *The opening of the 15th meeting of the leading group of the Central Committee on Comprehensive Deepening Reform.* www.gov.cn/xin wen/2015-08/18/content_2915043.htm. Accessed 1 July 2020.

Temple, J., Story, A., & Delaforce, W. H. (2005). *AUCEA: An emerging collaborative and strategic approach dedicated to university-community engagement in Australia.* www.engagementaustralia.org.au. Accessed 1 July 2020.

Tokyo Tech. (2017). *Report on performance evaluation result of fiscal year.* https://www.titech.ac.jp/about/disclosure/evaluation/pdf/28jissekihoukok usyo.pdf. Accessed 1 July 2020.

Webber, K. L., & Calderon, A. J. (2015). Institutional research, planning, and decision support in higher education today. In K. L. Webber & A. J. Calderon (Eds.), *Institutional research and planning in higher education.* Abingdon: Routledge.

Zhang, N., & Guo, N. (2014). An empirical study on the relation between capabilities of teaching and research for young faculty members. *Contemporary Teacher Education, 7*(2), 76–81.

Zhong, Z., Coates, H., & Shi, J. (Eds.). (2019a). *Innovations in Asian higher education.* Abingdon: Routledge.

Zhong, Z., Liu, L., Coates, H., & Kuh, G. (2019). What the US (and rest of the world) should know about higher education in China. *Change: The Magazine of Higher Learning, 51*(3), 8–20.

Zhou, P., Tijssen, R., & Leydesdorff, L. (2016). University-industry collaboration in China and the USA: A bibliometric comparison. *PLoS ONE, 11*(11), 1–18.

CHAPTER 5

From Energy Efficiency to Stakeholder Involvement and Beyond? Case Study on the Advancement of Sustainable Development at the University of Bremen

Bror Giesenbauer, Merle K. Tegeler, and Georg Müller-Christ

INTRODUCTION

In times of massive global disruption, universities and other higher education institutions (HEIs) are called to take responsibility for societal transformation (Barth & Rieckmann, 2016). In this chapter, we are going to explore how our own university, the University of Bremen, Germany, responds to the challenge of becoming a change agent.

B. Giesenbauer (✉) · M. K. Tegeler · G. Müller-Christ
University of Bremen, Bremen, Germany
e-mail: giesenbauer@uni-bremen.de

M. K. Tegeler
e-mail: tegeler@uni-bremen.de

G. Müller-Christ
e-mail: gmc@uni-bremen.de

© The Author(s), under exclusive license to Springer Nature
Switzerland AG 2021
L. Tauginienė and R. Pučėtaitė (eds.), *Managing Social Responsibility in Universities*, https://doi.org/10.1007/978-3-030-70013-3_5

HEIs have to react to global trends that are difficult to chase at the same time—and that indeed often impose conflicting goals. As success of HEIs is mostly measured by international rankings and leadership in specialized disciplines, the advancement of cross-cutting topics such as sustainable development (SD) is often compromised (Giesenbauer & Tegeler, 2020). Being part of the German research consortium on 'Sustainability at Higher Education Institutions' HOCH-N (Bassen, Schmitt, & Stecker, 2017), we have already explored in past publications (Giesenbauer, 2021; Giesenbauer & Müller-Christ, 2020; Giesenbauer & Tegeler, 2020) how HEIs could possibly come to integrate the pressing challenge of SD into their actions while also having to manage the challenges like internationalization, massification, marketization and digitalization (Altbach, 2008).

As the overarching theme of this chapter is the transformation of HEIs toward meeting the challenges of SD, the latter is shortly introduced in section "The Challenges of Sustainable Development and HEI Development". In order to set the stage for analyzing the implementation of SD at the University of Bremen, an encompassing theoretical framework for systemic development based on Clare W. Graves' (Beck & Cowan, 2006; Graves, 1974) theory of systemic evolution is introduced and applied to HEIs. The framework culminates in the idea of a University 4.0, functioning as an infrastructure platform for cross-sectoral communication, facilitating open science, and co-creative and effective problem solving.

The theoretical parts of this chapter are based on the open access publication on the idea of a University 4.0 by Giesenbauer and Müller-Christ (2020). A case study of the University of Bremen illustrates the proposed ideas on HEI development in the Results section, examining its activities with regards to SD based on the three published sustainability reports. The chapter closes with a discussion of possible next steps for the University of Bremen, of general conclusions for HEI development, and of the study's limitations.

The Challenges of Sustainable Development and HEI Development

How can higher education institutions live up to the challenge of sustainable development while also having to deal with complex issues such as internationalization, massification, or marketization (Altbach, 2008; Sadlak & Liu, 2007)? Following the reasoning of Otto Scharmer, HEIs would need to upgrade their "operating system" (cf. Scharmer, 2018) and to increase their network activities in order to integrate SD as a whole-institutional approach (Scharmer, 2019). But what is meant by sustainable development in higher education? And how can the upgrading of a HEI's operating system be understood?

In the following section the topic of SD is thus shortly introduced and linked to HEIs. Thereafter follows an overview of Clare Graves' systemic theories that have been applied successfully to the field of corporate sustainability and that are linked to managing increasingly complex challenges (Giesenbauer & Müller-Christ, 2018; Müller-Christ & Giesenbauer, 2019). Furthermore, Graves' model is applied to HEIs to set the stage for the analysis of the University of Bremen.

Sustainable Development in Higher Education

The famous publication of "Our Common Future" in 1987 by the World Commission on Environment and Development (1987) promoted the term "sustainable development" and gave birth to large global efforts to spread and develop the concept. Therein, SD is defined as "development that meets the needs of the present without compromising the ability of future generations to meet their own needs" (World Commission on Environment and Development, 1987, p. 41). SD should thus ensure that resources are built, grown or regenerated faster than they are used up, which is (a) often in conflict with short term goals and decisions and (b) increases the level of complexity as it expands the scope and time frame of decision making (Müller-Christ, 2011).

From the mid-1990s on researchers have conceptualized ways of implementing SD both as a concept and as a way of thinking at universities (Leal Filho, MacDermott, & Padgham, 1996; see, e.g., Barth & Rieckmann, 2016). Especially the adoption of the Sustainable Development Goals (SDGs) by the United Nations (2015) General Assembly and an increasing societal awareness of climate change have urged HEIs to integrate SD into their actions (Hugé, Block, Waas, Wright, & Dahdouh-Guebas, 2016). But even though the idea of SD has reached the general public—for example through Greta Thunberg and the *Fridays for Future* movement—the concept itself has not yet made it to mainstream academia (Blanco-Portela, Benayas, Pertierra, & Lozano, 2017; Mader, Scott, & Abdul Razak, 2013; Müller-Christ, Giesenbauer, & Tegeler, 2018; Thomas, 2004).

One of the reasons that SD has not made its way into mainstream academia and management of HEIs is likely to be found in its inherent complexity, as SD requires systemic transformation and not only adaptation (Bauer, Bormann, Kummer, Niedlich, & Rieckmann, 2018; Moore et al., 2005). In other words, taking the challenge of SD seriously will lead to more tensions and dilemmas and therefore to increased complexity (Lattu & Cai, 2020). Consequently, Bauer et al. (2018) argue that HEIs should implement SD as a whole-institution approach in order to encourage transformative practices at all levels. If a given HEI wants to get serious about integrating the idea of SD, it should therefore aim to build its capacity to deal with complexity and ambiguity and lean into a more integrative worldview, which will be explained and discussed below.

Worldviews and Systemic Development of HEIs

To understand complex systems such as universities and the field of higher education in general, it is helpful to build on a framework that is able to structure and explain the evolution of systems in general—the "upgrading of operating systems", as Scharmer coins it (cf. Scharmer, 2018). The psychologist Clare W. Graves developed such a systemic theory from the 1950s to the 1970s, trying to explain adult human development based on his own empirical data (Beck & Cowan, 2006; Graves, 1974, 2002). Graves distinguished eight distinct worldviews, also described as value systems, phases, or levels, that affect the general view of human beings on the world like a filter on a camera lens. His teachings were made popular in the 1990s under the name of *Spiral Dynamics* (Beck & Cowan, 2006).

Worldviews are usually shared by people within a similar group and thus the individual and collective development are intertwined. According to Graves, the worldview development of both individual adults and social systems oscillates in a spiral movement between worldviews that focus on the individual and worldviews that focus on the collective (Beck & Cowan, 2006; Graves, 1974; Van Marrewijk & Werre, 2003). The idea of a spiral development also implies that certain phases or worldviews cannot be skipped—they have to be run through sequentially, though different speeds and depths of development are possible. For example, universities are expected to start from a solid infrastructure and orderly formal settings for teaching and studying, to then go on to building capacities for high quality research and only later to champion transdisciplinary research focusing on solving relevant societal problems. However, when new institutions are founded they can build on the lessons from older institutions and speed their own development—especially compared to the systemic development of universities that were founded in medieval times with a focus on dissemination of factual knowledge.

Following the reasoning of Hedlund-de Witt (2014) only four worldviews from Graves' model will be discussed in detail and applied to HEIs, as the preceding three worldviews are more applicable to e.g. tribes, early empires, and mafia-type organizational forms and later worldviews are currently mostly expressed by individuals or in spiritual contexts.

While the descriptions below seem to imply a hierarchy of development and therefore dismiss "lower levels" of worldviews, all worldviews are inherently equally important. However, they can be more or less suited to handle different environmental conditions. Moreover, worldviews are often combined and can be temporarily adopted depending on the situational context. To complicate matters further, large systems such as HEIs are made up of a variety of subsystems which have their own unique combination and expression of worldviews. Nonetheless, we find that the four worldviews described below provide a helpful map for navigating the development of HEIs (Giesenbauer & Müller-Christ, 2020).

Systemic Development of Higher Education Institutions Toward Integrated Sustainability Governance

In the following, four types of worldviews in the systemic development of HEIs are shortly introduced, following the ideas of Müller-Christ (2017), Scharmer (2019, 2018), and Giesenbauer and Tegeler (2020). As these four HEI specific worldviews have historically evolved in a sequential manner, they are also described as phases of HEI development. Furthermore, as these phases can be described as major upgrades to the 'operating system' of a HEI (Scharmer, 2019), they are labelled with numbering from 1.0 to 4.0, following the nomenclature of software development.

Four Phases of HEI Development
Traditional/collegial HEI 1.0. Universities were historically invented from the catholic idea of preserving and teaching universal truths in medieval times (Fallis, 2007). A supposedly "all-knowing" scholar dressed in academic gown would then read his teachings to relatively passive

students, separated by strong disciplines. The impressiveness of large clas-
sicist university buildings as palaces of knowledge reflects this kind of
focus on authority, stability and persisting truths (Müller-Christ, 2017).
In general, a traditional HEI 1.0 will be focused on teaching, basic
research, and technological transfer. Its sustainability governance can then
be described as a one-dimensional approach, compliant to regulation, e.g.
with respect to waste management and safety.

The prototypical HEI 1.0 might seem outdated and yet has succeeded
in preserving academic education for several centuries. Indeed, its worldview still influences the ethos of modern universities—based on the
systemic principle of *transcend and include* (Van Marrewijk & Werre,
2003; Wilber, 2001). By itself, a traditional HEI or University 1.0 is
not likely to integrate fast-paced societal change and address cross-cutting
topics such as SD as a whole, as these topics demand more openness,
dialogue and at least some degree of interdisciplinarity. However, even
traditional universities had to adapt to societal change following the Age
of Enlightenment and the rise of modern democracy.

Modern/metric-focused HEI 2.0. Universities were reinvented in
Germany in the nineteenth century by Wilhelm von Humboldt and
others as research universities (Kerr, 2001), which were later adapted
into the American model—combining the German research idea with the
English collegiate tradition and the American idea of service to society (cf.
Altbach, 2008, p. 8). As an early expression of the modern worldview, it
focused on the research *process*, allowing for more fluidity, and leading to
the idea of continuous improvement and process optimization. The rise
of the research university model enabled massive breakthroughs in terms
of research methods, standards of publication, and historic innovations
for civilization in fields such as technology, engineering, and medicine.

Current academia is mainly shaped by this reinvention of higher
education in light of the modern worldview. Quantification, professional
specialization and competition form the basis for most endeavors of HEIs.
HEIs 2.0 compete for grants, students and placements in rankings—and
thus in short for quantitative success (Altbach & Levy, 2005; Sadlak &
Liu, 2007). This orientation toward quantitative success is amplified by
the trends of massification (as participation in higher education growths
on national and international levels), globalization and internationalization, and leads to increased marketization and privatization (Altbach,
2008; Altbach, Reisberg, & Rumbley, 2010). Consequently, teaching
has become test-centric and modularized and HEIs have come to adopt

entrepreneurial activities. Furthermore, scientific careers can nearly exclusively be advanced within disciplinary niches based on metrics such as numbers of publications and impact factors, hindering the advancement of interdisciplinary fields and cross-cutting topics such as SD (Giesenbauer & Tegeler, 2020). These trends seem to intensify at the moment even though there are parallel lines of developments.

Over-all, a modern HEI 2.0 will be focused on quantitative growth and rapid growth in functional buildings with little energy awareness. It regards SD as a management task and tries to tackle SD issues by controlling cash flows and process management.

Postmodern/responsibility-focused HEI 3.0. The main alternative development of higher education is currently shaped by a postmodern worldview, especially in the social sciences and humanities. Dismissing positivism and objectivism, the subjective viewpoints from both research participants and students stand at the center of research and education at postmodern HEIs. Seminars, project work and qualitative research methods have been developed in the spirit of this HEI 3.0. Learning arrangements are then focused on competencies rather than on knowledge accumulation only (Rieckmann, 2012). These developments occurred together with student movements from about the 1950s, protesting against patriarchal hierarchies of HEI 1.0 and the somewhat mechanical teaching styles of HEI 1.0 and 2.0. This type of postmodern HEI or University 3.0 has brought about a focus on societal issues such as SD and led to the rise of interdisciplinary research. Researchers operating from a postmodern worldview will usually try to make everyone heard and to include regional and international stakeholders (Leal Filho, 2010). However, researchers often have to play by the rules of the modern worldview of HEI 2.0 in order to advance their careers, leading to trade-offs and tensions on a personal level (Giesenbauer & Tegeler, 2020, p. 645).

In general, a postmodern HEI 3.0 will focus on facilitating lively communities and individual expression, championing diversity management and the goal of climate neutrality. SD is then seen as a community task and third mission content (Niedlich, Kummer, Bauer, Rieckmann, & Bormann, 2019).

Integrative/engaged HEI 4.0. As conventional ways of decision making and education (including postmodern dialogical practices) are put under pressure by increasingly fast-paced and complex societal changes in times of globalization and digitalization, some parts of HEIs have come to adopt novel practices in line with the integrative worldview. Experiences from smaller academic projects and other organizational forms (e.g. businesses) operating from an integrative worldview allow for preliminary descriptions of this emerging type of HEI.

Integrative HEIs 4.0 will likely exhibit a focus on self-management, a strive for wholeness, as well as an awareness of their evolutionary purpose, taking responsibility and trying to actively participate in societal change (Giesenbauer & Tegeler, 2020; Laloux, 2014). Taking systems as a whole into perspective, the co-creation of effective solutions for pressing societal issues such as SD will be emphasized in HEIs 4.0. Based on Graves' model of systemic development, Universities or HEIs 4.0 are bound to act as brokers for integrative processes, facilitating synergies between different societal sectors.

Building almost exclusively on Russian research and philosophical works, Alla Lapteva and Varlerii Efimov come to very similar conclusions and conceptualize a University 4.0 as "an infrastructure platform" for a variety of activities (Lapteva & Efimov, 2016, p. 2691). Focusing on the technical basis for HEI development, analogous to the waves of industrial revolution, Lapteva and Efimov stress the importance of telecommunication technologies for Universities 4.0. Thus, HEIs become, "a very open environment – a hub for a variety of communications, a node at the intersection of multiple networks (...). These communications, research works and development projects involve not only professors and students, but also a wide range of external participants" (Lapteva & Efimov, 2016, p. 2691).

Consequently, new concepts for higher education such as the living lab approach (Verhoef & Bossert, 2019) are built around the idea of inclusive and dynamic research processes. The inclusion of students and citizens in the research process is intended to facilitate deep learning and to link research with education, knowledge transfer and real-life application (Schneidewind, 2014). And even without direct field testing of ideas, research-based learning and co-creative innovation methods can be applied in courses. At the very least, learners should be encouraged to personally engage with sustainability and to learn by *experiencing* and *becoming aware*—going beyond mere cognitive processing (Murray, Goodhew, & Murray, 2014).

Emphasizing the transformative aspect of HEI development, Otto Scharmer and Katrin Kaufer propose that learning at integrative HEIs 4.0 will be shaped by action learning, global classrooms, innovation hubs, and individualized lifelong learning journeys (Scharmer & Kaufer, 2013).

Scharmer goes on to argue in two blog posts, that the university of the twenty-first century should in essence focus on providing *vertical development literacy*, i.e. the ability to understand systems and their respective worldviews, and to guide these systems through a systemic upgrade, if needed (Scharmer, 2018). According to Scharmer (2019) this leading of transformative change requires among others the skill of "deep listening", self-awareness, and compassion.

Similarly, Schneidewind (2013) proposes that HEIs should focus on facilitating *transformative literacy*, i.e. the ability to understand and participate in social transformation. SD will then supposedly not be a special topic to deal with, but an integral part of a HEIs DNA and governance, following the whole-institution approach (Giesenbauer & Tegeler, 2020; Vogt & Weber, 2020). Interestingly, the qualitative data from a multi-case study by Niedlich et al. (2019) suggest a linear relationship between the orientation toward organizational learning of a given HEI and the degree of holistic orientation of its sustainability governance, supporting the general assumption that the development of HEIs from 1.0 to 4.0 equals a general systemic upgrade—going beyond incremental and isolated updates.

Leading Multi-level Development of HEIs
The presented four phases of systemic HEI development are intended to provide a map for navigating the transformation of HEIs in the twenty-first century. In times of increasing complexity and a "knowing-doing gap", as Scharmer (2019) coins it, HEIs would do well to prepare for a systemic upgrade in order to keep up with societal demands, specifically the challenge of SD. Currently HEIs around the world are at very different stages of development, described as stratification of higher education (Stensaker et al., 2019). We would go one step further and argue that each HEI in itself is stratified as is, as different organizational subsystems emphasize different worldviews and exhibit different levels of maturity within a given worldview. Transformation would thus necessitate a consciously chosen multi-level approach.

As most HEIs are expected to be centered around the traditional 1.0 or modern 2.0 worldviews, the next step would likely be one of strengthening the ideas of quality control (traditional/collegial worldview) and process optimization (modern/metric-focused worldview), while also championing dialogical forms of research and education (postmodern/responsibility-focused worldview). Inspiration for taking the predominant HEI 2.0 one step further can be found in J. G. Wissema's *3GU* model (Wissema, 2009), mainly with regards to restructuring HEIs—enabling more interdisciplinary research in institutes, professionalizing HEI management and promoting entrepreneurial activities and outreach.

In sum, the integration of more participatory, open, and transdisciplinary practices should be encouraged at all levels while simultaneously consolidating methodological rigor and effective process management—rethinking prevalent ways of HEI organization. In this way, a University or HEI 4.0 will become an infrastructure platform for cross-sectoral communication, facilitating open science and co-creative problem solving. In the Results section we will discuss how the University of Bremen is trying to manage its systemic development with respect to SD.

METHODS

It is our understanding that all sound empirical research needs to be built on sound conceptual models and sound operationalization thereof. Thus, this contribution is intended to advance theory building on the transformation of higher education by systematically applying Clare W. Graves' model of systemic evolution to sustainable higher education development.

A case study of the University of Bremen illustrates the proposed ideas on HEI development. This case study focuses on the historic development of SD related activities at the University of Bremen. It is not intended to "prove" the preceding conceptual framework, as case studies are not suited to falsify conceptualizations in a classic way. However, the main scientific contribution of a case study can be described as "case-inspired self-reflection" (Wals, Walker, & Corcoran, 2004, p. 347). In this sense, the case study on the University of Bremen is intended to illustrate the practical application of the systemic theories at hand, to validate their subjective *usefulness*, and to inspire ideas for application in the reader.

The case study of the University of Bremen is based on a document analysis of the available sustainability reports covering the period from 2000 to 2015. The analysis grid used is based on the four levels of ambition that were described above. To carry out a systemic document analysis, all three sustainability reports of the university were used to filter out the existing projects and initiatives as the first step of the analysis. Subsequently, different categories were formed based on the four different levels of HEI development. Each of the four different categories was described with a summary sentence so that the individual projects and initiatives could be filtered accordingly (Schmidt, 2017, p. 450):

- HEI 1.0: "Focused on teaching, basic research, basic technological transfer, and legal compliance"
- HEI 2.0: "Regarding sustainable development as a management task, focusing on energy-efficiency and resource flows"
- HEI 3.0: "Reaching out to various stakeholders and focusing on competencies and responsibility"
- HEI 4.0: "Becoming an infrastructure platform for cross-sectoral communication, facilitating open science and co-creative problem solving"

The four categories described served as an analytical grid to classify the different projects and initiatives of development at the University of Bremen. Two researchers discussed the classification and the third author reviewed it. While true researcher triangulation would have been preferable, this process allowed us to work around significant time constraints.

Results

Overview Over the Sustainability Reports of the University of Bremen

The University of Bremen was founded in 1971 in Bremen, Northern Germany, and has come to be one of the larger universities with more than 20,000 students. From about the year 2000 it started to build structures for sustainability management which were displayed in three sustainability reports, covering the years 2000–2005, 2006–2010, and 2011–2015, respectively. The reports summarize a wide range of activities and lay out next steps without providing key indicators.

As the University of Bremen was founded on the premise of social responsibility, its philosophy has always been close to the concept of SD. The fundamental understanding of SD is based on the three pillars of sustainability, namely the ecological, economic, and social dimensions. All three pillars are supposed to be equally important in their implementation at the University of Bremen and are integrated into the organization through different channels.

The three sustainability reports (Universität Bremen, 2005, 2010, 2015) do not distinguish between the individual pillars, but rather between different levels of ambition and targeted domains of the various initiatives at the University of Bremen. A short summary of each report is given below.

The first report gives an overview over basic activities, mostly dealing with managing internal matters. For example, a climate protection concept was implemented at the university, mainly focusing on operations. Furthermore, the report addresses the thematic focus on social issues in research and education. Additionally, the University of Bremen implemented a diversity strategy, including close thematic links between the thematic priorities of gender equality and SD, reflecting the SD concept of the University of Bremen (Universität Bremen, 2005).

The report covering 2006–2010 is focused on the area of ecological sustainability. The university has set itself the goal of becoming a climate-neutral university and thus becoming more energy- and resource-efficient. This goal is supposed to be supported by including SD in academic teaching. Here, the University of Bremen presents itself pursuing two different approaches. On the one hand, by fostering the exchange between faculties, students, and society within the framework of the university-wide Environmental Days, and on the other hand by merging the SD and digitalization strategies. In the context of the eGeneral Studies, courses have been created that deal with the topic of SD from different perspectives, accessible to all students (Universität Bremen, 2010).

The third report focused on the domain of social sustainability, e.g. by promoting inclusion of disability in doctorate programs. The University of Bremen is also assuming responsibility in the context of the growing refugee crisis and has launched a variety of related projects. In addition to social sustainability, the quality of teaching and the international orientation are highlighted to be central themes of the University of Bremen's efforts (Universität Bremen, 2015).

The overall reporting period covers the years 2000 to 2015 and represents a wide range of activities. Of course, the University of Bremen's commitment does not end with the reporting period described above. Especially the BMBF-funded project HOCH-N (standing for "sustainability in higher education"), has created a high visibility since 2016, together with the Virtual Academy of Sustainability, and also the implementation of a permanent committee on SD (Bassen et al., 2017; Schleker & Giesenbauer, 2019).

Results of the Analysis of the Systemic Development of the University of Bremen

The analysis scheme of the four levels of HEI development (see Methods section) was used to classify the activities gather from the three sustainability reports. Table 5.1 shows an overview of the activities of the University of Bremen over the publication period from 2000 to 2015, classified by HEI model, i.e. the presumed underlying worldview with regards to SD and HEI management. In line with the reasoning of section "Systemic Development of Higher Education Institutions toward Integrated Sustainability Governance", most of these activities are aligned with the postmodern worldview of HEI 3.0.

Table 5.1 Overview of SD related activities at the University of Bremen and their underlying HEI model.

Historically the University of Bremen started with more tangible and actionable issues, mostly dealing with the environmental aspects of sustainable development. This includes water and waste management, greening the campus, and installation of solar panels. These types of activities are great entry points for sustainability management as they can even be implemented when leadership is more inclined with HEI 2.0 or even 1.0. The main pivot seems to be the implementation of EMAS, the Eco Management and Audit Scheme from the European Union, in 2004. Only after the resource management was professionalized did the University of Bremen start a more general top-down sustainability governance, illustrated by the installment of permanent committee for sustainability in 2017. We propose that this pattern can be observed at other HEIs as well.

Besides these more top down implemented activities with regards to environmental aspects, a lot of smaller scale projects with regards to the social aspects of SD were founded. Most of these projects were designed to increase inclusivity and diversity at the university, both with respect to students and personnel, and can be classified as expressions of a bottom-up HEI 3.0. As universities are usually made up of relatively independent departments, they should encourage these kinds of activities and later help to solidify the learnings.

Table 5.1 Overview of SD related activities at the University of Bremen and their underlying HEI model

Reporting period	HEI model	Activity
2010–2015	1.0	Publication of basic informational material on SD
2000–2005	1.0	Networking in fund raising—collecting donations for scientific projects
2000–2005	1.0–2.0	Sponsored by the economy—The Chair of Innovative Brand Management (LiM)
2005–2015	1.0–3.0	Quality improvement in teaching—establishment of an online-supported quality management portal for self-observation and further development of study programs – > cooperation between study programs
2010–2015	1.0–3.0	Quality management in teaching and the system accreditation of the university—departments reflect their study programs and introduce new procedures for quality management, e.g. "European Quality Audit"
2010–2015	1.0–3.0	Studying with a handicap—accessibility, participation and challenges—the Interest Group Handicap (IGH) continues to work for the renovation of buildings for accessibility
2000–2015	2.0	The integrated climate protection concept and its scope—new guidelines for climate protection at the university and creation of a catalogue of measures; implementation of the measures
2000–2005	2.0	Development of the Career Center—Career advice from a place where students are advised
2000–2015	2.0	Promoting research—increasing the visibility of the university through the German Excellence Initiative, promotion of doctoral programs, interface development with industry, junior professorships
2005–2015	2.0	Partnerships with business and society—promotion of funds in research
2010–2015	2.0	The international orientation of the university: Development of objectives to promote foreign students at the university and cooperation with other HEIs
2005–2010	2.0	ESD in teacher training—further support for sustainable student companies and student shops, children's cafés; in addition, several workshops and offers for teacher training

(continued)

Table 5.1   (continued)

Reporting period	HEI model	Activity
2000–2005	2.0	Overall energy optimization and modernization of Bremen State and University Library—Building renovation and environmental plan
2005–2015	2.0	EMAS at the University of Bremen—efforts to institutionalize environmental protection are constantly being further developed within the framework of EMAS
2010–2015	2.0–3.0	Model project: InWi—Inclusion in Science—financial support for 12 severely disabled doctoral students
2005–2010	2.0–3.0	UniUmwelttage at the University of Bremen—further appointments of environmental days for discourse on environmental topics with students and the general public
2005–2010	2.0–3.0	Environmental awareness—reducing IT energy consumption, making building management more sustainable through effective use of rainwater
2010–2015	2.0–3.0	Reduction of CO_2 emissions—suggestions for mobility management—surveys on the use of public transportation and the use of bicycles
2010–2015	3.0	Science meets school—cooperation with schools. Pupils may attend lectures
2000–2015	3.0	Family-friendly university—establishment of an audit, improvement of working time organization through discussions with the faculties, more flexible study and examination regulations for students with family obligations, childcare during the summer and autumn holidays
2000–2015	3.0	Ensuring sustainable quality in teaching—Example: Students work more in seminars to reflexively discuss social and SD issues (e.g. SDGs)
2000–2015	3.0	Recognizing and supporting social diversity—developing a diversity strategy, increasing support for minorities, setting up advice centers, etc.
2000–2015	3.0	Gender-equitable and sustainable—new objectives for equal opportunities and the prevention of discrimination against women and others, recognition of the high percentage of female employees
2010–2015	3.0	Implementing education for sustainable development with innovative learning formats—four-tube academy to combine classroom teaching with online teaching

(continued)

Table 5.1 (continued)

Reporting period	HEI model	Activity
2010–2015	3.0	From the UN Decade and the World Action Programme on ESD to the University of Bremen—conferences are held on the topic of ESD
2010–2015	3.0	Pilot project "Fit in MINT"—Reintegration of the long-term unemployed and people on family leave. Maintenance of further training courses and seminars
2005–2010	3.0	Research project northwest 2050—development of the "Roadmap of Change" in cooperation with partners from economy, politics and society
2000–2010	3.0	SD and environmental protection in scientific courses—Maintenance and expansion of the range of courses related to sustainability
2005–2010	3.0	Sustainability events for all: eGeneral Studies—combination of online teaching (eGeneral Studies) with classroom teaching to ensure sustainable development of education
2000–2010	3.0	Promoting health resources—reducing burdens—publication of the framework concept for occupational health management, preparation of the first health report, commissioning of the processing of further fields of action of the framework concept, organization of a health day
2005–2010	3.0–4.0	Students research for sustainable development at the University of Bremen—Permanent involvement of students in sustainability-related research
2005–2010	3.0–4.0	The University of Bremen on the way to becoming a climate-neutral university—expansion of energy-saving measures, e.g. by optimizing ventilation, heat recovery and compressed air generation systems and optimization of the lighting system
2010–2015	4.0	University and students show commitment to refugees—recognition of voluntary help in the escape and integration of refugees. Can be credited as a course
2010–2015	4.0	German Action Days on SD at the University of Bremen—finding solutions for problems of SD and discourse

Most of the examples above are focused on operations and campus management as well as on outreach and networking. At least in the case of the University of Bremen, these kinds of activities are easier to implement than to increase the inclusion of SD in teaching or research. However, some best practices for increasing the visibility of SD in teaching and research can be derived from the case of the University of Bremen.

First of all, members of the University of Bremen recognized early on that the topic of SD could be included in the so-called General Studies and especially the eGeneral Studies program of the University. Both students at the bachelor's and master's level have some leeway to sign up for courses not related to their main program. Therefore, the creation of online courses on SD via the Virtual Academy of Sustainability (Schleker & Giesenbauer, 2019) enables the University to potentially reach all 22,000 students with lectures and seminars on diverse aspects of SD, independent of time and location. In the lectures, learning goals are formulated and suggestions for self-study are made. Courses are designed for students of all fields of study and levels. Students can write an electronic exam on demand in the university's test center: they choose the date of the exam fitting their schedule. The concept of eGeneral Studies also allows these courses to be viewed by students from other universities and all those interested in university continuing education (Universität Bremen, 2010).

The solution of implementing the topic of SD in freely available online courses represents a major lever for education for sustainable development (ESD). Thus, it serves the HEI 3.0 mindset (taking responsibility and being inclusive), while also fitting the HEI 2.0 mindset by being efficient and scalable, all the while preparing the ground for more a HEI 4.0 where sustainability is regarded as a given and the basis for effective solutions. The Corona crisis has highlighted the importance of digital learning structures and thus the general concept of the Virtual Academy of Sustainability could help other HEIs to both work on promoting SD and increasing organizational resilience.

Another best practice can be found in the general commitment of networking with other institutions, be they business partners, NGOs, other HEIs or civic organizations. Engaging with these stakeholders prepares the ground for HEI 3.0 and 4.0, as the complex topics of SD and social responsibility can only be tackled by joint forces and co-creative problem solving.

DISCUSSION

In general, the results show a strong focus on activities that seem to be in line with HEI 2.0 and 3.0. However, some of the activities that were classified as HEI 2.0 might well be *operated* from a mindset of a modern worldview of HEI 3.0 and vice versa. For example, the idea that the University should be mindful of its energy and resource flows with a systematic approach like EMAS is likely an expression of HEI 3.0 and facilitates more awareness and discussion about environmental concerns on the campus. The operation of such an approach is more a matter of professionalization and process management, more in line with the thinking of HEI 2.0. Overall, most activities related to SD seem to be related to the mindset of HEI 3.0 with few examples of integrative HEI 4.0 practices. However, from our observation, the general focus of the University of Bremen seems to be laid upon strengthening the professionalism and internationalism of HEI 2.0. Therefore, we do not expect a quick transition to the general University 4.0 model, at least not on an organizational level.

Looking at the University of Bremen's development, several possible next steps can be outlined in light of the University 4.0 model (see section "Systemic Development of Higher Education Institutions toward Integrated Sustainability Governance"). First of all, the variety of different activities could be bundled, and synergies promoted. In general, it would be advisable to first solidify what has been developed more or less organically, in line with the professional attitude of HEI 2.0. Meanwhile, the growth and development of further smaller scale activities should be encouraged, helping to build an inclusive campus in line with HEI 3.0 and 4.0. The framework of the SDGs could help to bundle these diverse activities under the general umbrella of sustainable development and to inspire new activities. Moreover, networking activities should be encouraged (see Giesenbauer & Müller-Christ, 2020).

Furthermore, the content of SD could be promoted by making the SDGs more known throughout the University, by creating more courses related to the topic, by requiring every student to attend at least one course on the subject, and by creating new focal points on SD, for example when assigning new professors.

We propose that a conscious multi-level approach, providing both more structure and encouraging independent bottom-up initiatives would help to solidify previous achievements and to prepare the ground for further development. Professionalizing the management of SD (HEI 2.0) and increasing networking activities and cross-sectoral collaboration (HEI 3.0 and 4.0) are among the next steps. The concept of the SDGs might help with both endeavors by highlighting commonalities and simplifying communication. Moreover, education should increasingly be understood as a means of personal development and developing the skill of co-creative problem solving in order to facility the rise HEI 4.0.

The case of the University of Bremen illustrates the complexity of becoming a change agent. On the one hand, the university is a strong change agent when it comes to areas such as operations and supporting individual members realizing SD related projects. On the other hand, these efforts are not fully integrated and thus lack the creative power and problem-solving capabilities that are conceptualized in the idea of a University 4.0. For example, if the process managing idea is taken seriously, more measurements of key indicators might be needed, also for areas of social impact. However, benchmarking is only useful when an organization is willing to change course according to the data. In the case of the University of Bremen this would mean unequivocal support by the top management as well as openness of the relatively independent faculties. To achieve this kind of support it would probably be advisable to foster inter-organizational communications and participation. Only then could the University of Bremen live up to is potential, build on its achievements and move toward an integrated University 4.0.

Overall, we have found the analysis grid helpful in reflecting the recent history of SD activities at the University of Bremen. The case study exemplifies that, while the University 4.0 model might be more effective and even wished for in times of global disruption, each HEI has to start where it is—and thus should start by taking an honest look at its status quo—in order to enable organic systemic development toward the implementation of SD. The proposed model of HEI development can help to structure the diversity of activities and to outline reasonable next steps. In this way, this chapter is intended to shed some light on possible paths of HEI development in the context of SD and thus to help HEIs to deal with increasing complexity.

However, the case study is not without limitations. First of all, as a single case study it should not be generalized hastily. Moreover, reports have the weakness of being less critical as they are usually used for promotion purposes too. Thus, the data basis for the analysis has the potential of being biased and not representative—for example by possibly omitting activities that could be regarded to be in conflict with SD. Additionally, the case is likely to be shaped by the specificities of the German higher education system, e.g. the relatively high autonomy of research and education and the tradition of public funding. Similarly, the University of

Bremen is a relatively young and yet large university with a focus on social responsibility and less rigid top-down management and therefore findings might not apply to older or more conservative institutions.

More research would be needed to (a) refine the University 4.0 model, (b) study true examples of the proposed HEI 4.0 level, (c) operationalize the levels of HEI development in general, and (d) shed light on developmental paths and best practices for managing the systemic development of HEIs. As we deem the prospect of a University 4.0 as a change agent in times of global disruption and complexity as promising, this type of research could play a vital role in the realization of SD and the SDGs–in higher education and society in general.

References

Altbach, P. G. (2008). The complex roles of universities in the period of globalization. In Global University Network for Innovation (GUNI) (Eds.), *Higher education in the world 3—Higher education: New challenges and emerging roles for human and social development* (Higher Education in the World, Vol. 3, pp. 5–14). London: Palgrave Macmillan.

Altbach, P. G., & Levy, D. C. (Eds.). (2005). *Private higher education: A global revolution* (Global Perspectives on Higher Education, Vol. 2). Rotterdam: Sense Publishers.

Altbach, P. G., Reisberg, L., & Rumbley, L. (2010). *Trends in global higher education: Tracking an academic revolution* (Global Perspectives on Higher Education, Vol. 22). Rotterdam: Sense Publishers; UNESCO Publishing.

Barth, M., & Rieckmann, M. (2016). State of the art in research on higher education for sustainable development. In M. Barth, G. Michelsen, M. Rieckmann, & I. Thomas (Eds.), *Routledge handbook of higher education for sustainable development* (Routledge International Handbooks, pp. 100–113). London: Routledge; Earthscan from Routledge.

Bassen, A., Schmitt, C. T., & Stecker, C. (2017). Nachhaltigkeit an Hochschulen: entwickeln – vernetzen – berichten (HOCH-N). *uwf (UmweltWirtschaftsForum), 25*, 139–146. https://doi.org/10.1007/s00550-017-0450-y.

Bauer, M., Bormann, I., Kummer, B., Niedlich, S., & Rieckmann, M. (2018). Sustainability governance at universities: Using a governance equalizer as a research heuristic. *Higher Education Policy, 31*, 491–511. https://doi.org/10.1057/s41307-018-0104-x.

Beck, D., & Cowan, C. C. (2006). *Spiral dynamics: Mastering values, leadership and change: Exploring the new science of memetics.* Malden, MA: Blackwell.

Blanco-Portela, N., Benayas, J., Pertierra, L. R., & Lozano, R. (2017). The integration of sustainability in higher education institutions: A review of drivers of and barriers to organisational change and their comparison against those found of companies. *Journal of Cleaner Production, 166,* 563–578.

Fallis, G. (2007). *Multiversities, ideas, and democracy* (2nd ed.). Toronto: University of Toronto Press.

Giesenbauer, B. (2021). Veränderung durch Veränderung: Nachhaltige Entwicklung von Hochschulen im Huckepack der Digitalisierung. In W. Leal Filho (Ed.), *Theorie und Praxis der Nachhaltigkeit. Digitalisierung und Nachhaltigkeit* (pp. 45–63). Springer Spektrum. https://doi.org/10.1007/978-3-662-61534-8_3.

Giesenbauer, B., & Müller-Christ, G. (2018). Mit den Sustainable Development Goals zu einer sinnhaften und nachhaltigen Unternehmensführung?: Systemische Evolutionsstufen als Unterscheidungsmerkmal für unterschiedliche Zugänge von Unternehmen. In H. Rogall, H. C. Binswanger, F. Ekardt, A. Grothe, W.-D. Hasenclever, I. Hauchler, et al. (Eds.), *Im Brennpunkt: Zukunft des nachhaltigen Wirtschaftens in der digitalen Welt* (Jahrbuch nachhaltige Ökonomie, 6.2018/2019, pp. 281–294). Marburg: Metropolis Verlag.

Giesenbauer, B., & Müller-Christ, G. (2020). University 4.0: Promoting the transformation of higher education institutions toward sustainable development. *Sustainability, 12,* 3371. https://doi.org/10.3390/su12083371.

Giesenbauer, B., & Tegeler, M. (2020). The transformation of higher education institutions towards sustainability from a systemic perspective. In W. Leal Filho, A. L. Salvia, R. W. Pretorius, L. L. Brandli, E. Manolas, F. Alves, et al. (Eds.), *Universities as living labs for sustainable development* (pp. 637–650). Cham: Springer International Publishing.

Graves, C. W. (1974). Human nature prepares for a momentous leap. *The Futurist, 8*(2), 72–87.

Graves, C. W. (2002). *Levels of human existence: Transcription of a seminar at the Washington School of Psychiatry, October 16, 1971.* Santa Barbara, CA: ECLET Publishing.

Hedlund-de Witt, A. (2014). Rethinking sustainable development: Considering how different worldviews envision "development" and "quality of life". *Sustainability, 6,* 8310–8328. https://doi.org/10.3390/su6118310.

Hugé, J., Block, T., Waas, T., Wright, T., & Dahdouh-Guebas, F. (2016). How to walk the talk? Developing actions for sustainability in academic research. *Journal of Cleaner Production, 137,* 83–92. https://doi.org/10.1016/j.jclepro.2016.07.010.

Kerr, C. (2001). *The uses of the university: With a new chapter and preface* (5th ed., Godkin Lectures). Cambridge, MA: Harvard University Press.

Laloux, F. (2014). *Reinventing organizations: A guide to creating organizations inspired by the next stage of human consciousness.* Brussels, Belgium: Nelson Parker.

Lapteva, A. V., & Efimov, V. S. (2016). New generation of universities. University 4.0. *Journal of Siberian Federal University. Humanities & Social Sciences, 11*, 2681–2696. https://doi.org/10.17516/1997-1370-2016-9-11-2681-2696.

Lattu, A., & Cai, Y. (2020). Tensions in the sustainability of higher education—The case of finnish universities. *Sustainability, 12*, 1941. https://doi.org/10.3390/su12051941.

Leal Filho, W. (2010). Teaching sustainable development at university level: Current trends and future needs. *Journal of Baltic Science Education, 9*(4), 273–284.

Leal Filho, W., MacDermott, F., & Padgham, J. (Eds.). (1996). *Implementing sustainable development at university level: A manual of good practice.* Bradford: European Research and Training Centre on Environmental Education.

Mader, C., Scott, G., & Abdul Razak, D. (2013). Effective change management, governance and policy for sustainability transformation in higher education. *Sustainability Accounting, Management and Policy Journal, 4*, 264–284. https://doi.org/10.1108/SAMPJ-09-2013-0037.

Moore, J., Pagani, F., Quayle, M., Robinson, J., Sawada, B., Spiegelman, G., et al. (2005). Recreating the university from within. *International Journal of Sustainability in Higher Education, 6*, 65–80. https://doi.org/10.1108/14676370510573140.

Müller-Christ, G. (2011). *Sustainable management: Coping with the dilemmas of resource-oriented management.* Berlin, Heidelberg: Springer-Verlag.

Müller-Christ, G. (2017). Nachhaltigkeitsforschung in einer transzendenten Entwicklung des Hochschulsystems – ein Ordnungsangebot für Innovativität. In W. Leal Filho (Ed.), *Innovation in der Nachhaltigkeitsforschung: Ein Beitrag zur Umsetzung der UNO Nachhaltigkeitsziele* (Theorie und Praxis der Nachhaltigkeit, Vol. 22, pp. 161–180). Berlin, Heidelberg: Springer Berlin Heidelberg.

Müller-Christ, G., & Giesenbauer, B. (2019). Integrales Ressourcenmanagement: Leitplanken einer nachhaltigkeitsbezogenen Möglichkeitswissenschaft. In L. Hochmann, S. Graupe, T. Korbun, S. Panther, & U. Schneidewind (Eds.), *Möglichkeitswissenschaften: Ökonomie mit Möglichkeitssinn* (pp. 307–332). Marburg: Metropolis Verlag.

Müller-Christ, G., Giesenbauer, B., & Tegeler, M. K. (2018). Die Umsetzung der SDGs im deutschen Bildungssystem – Studie im Auftrag des Rats für Nachhaltige Entwicklung der Bundesregierung. *Zeitschrift für internationale Bildungsforschung und Entwicklungspädagogik, 41*(2), 19–26.

Murray, P., Goodhew, J., & Murray, S. (2014). The heart of ESD: Personally engaging learners with sustainability. *Environmental Education Research, 20*, 718–734. https://doi.org/10.1080/13504622.2013.836623.

Niedlich, S., Kummer, B., Bauer, M., Rieckmann, M., & Bormann, I. (2019). Cultures of sustainability governance in higher education institutions: A multi-case study of dimensions and implications. *Higher Education Quarterly, 00,* 1–18. https://doi.org/10.1111/hequ.12237.

Rieckmann, M. (2012). Future-oriented higher education: Which key competencies should be fostered through university teaching and learning? *Futures, 44,* 127–135. https://doi.org/10.1016/j.futures.2011.09.005.

Sadlak, J., & Liu, N. C. (Eds.). (2007). *The world-class university and ranking: Aiming beyond status.* Bucharest: UNESCO-CEPES.

Scharmer, C. O. (2018, January 5). Education is the kindling of a flame: How to reinvent the 21st-century university. *HuffPost.* https://www.huffingto npost.com/entry/education-is-the-kindling-of-a-flame-how-to-reinvent_us_ 5a4ffec5e4b0ee59d41c0a9f. Accessed 25 March 2019.

Scharmer, C. O. (2019, April 16). Vertical literacy: Reimagining the 21st-Century University. *Medium.* https://medium.com/presencing-institute-blog/vertical-literacy-12-principles-for-reinventing-the-21st-century-univer sity-39c2948192ee. Accessed 2 May 2019.

Scharmer, C. O., & Kaufer, K. (2013). *Leading from the emerging future: From ego-system to eco-system economies* (1st ed.). San Francisco, CA: Berrett-Koehler.

Schleker, L., & Giesenbauer, B. (2019). Potenziale der digitalen Vermittlung der Sustainable Development Goals in der Hochschullehre. In W. Leal Filho (Ed.), *Aktuelle Ansätze zur Umsetzung der UN Nachhaltigkeitsziele.* Berlin: Springer Spektrum.

Schmidt, W. (2017). Dokumentenanalyse in der Organisationsforschung. In S. Liebig, W. Matiaske, & S. Rosenbohm (Eds.), *Handbuch Empirische Organisationsforschung* (Springer Reference Wirtschaft, pp. 443–466). Wiesbaden: Springer Fachmedien Wiesbaden.

Schneidewind, U. (2013). Transformative Literacy. Gesellschaftliche Veränderungsprozesse verstehen und gestalten. *GAIA—Ecological Perspectives on Science and Society, 22*(2), 82–86.

Schneidewind, U. (2014). Von der nachhaltigen zur transformativen Hochschule: Perspektiven einer "True University Sustainability". *Umwelt Wirtschafts Forum, 22*(4), 221–225.

Stensaker, B., Lee, J. J., Rhoades, G., Ghosh, S., Castiello-Gutiérrez, S., Vance, H., ..., Peel, C. (2019). Stratified university strategies: The shaping of institutional legitimacy in a global perspective. *The Journal of Higher Education, 90,* 539–562. https://doi.org/10.1080/00221546.2018.1513306.

Thomas, I. (2004). Sustainability in tertiary curricula: What is stopping it happening? *International Journal of Sustainability in Higher Education, 5*(1), 33–47.

United Nations. (2015). *Transforming our world: The 2030 agenda for sustainable development*. A/RES/70/1. New York. https://sustainabledevelopment. un.org/post2015/transformingourworld. Accessed 25 March 2019.

Universität Bremen. (2005). *Nachhaltigkeitsbericht 2000–2005*. Bremen.

Universität Bremen. (2010). *Nachhaltigkeitsbericht 2006–2010*. Bremen.

Universität Bremen. (2015). *Nachhaltigkeitsbericht 2011–2015*. Bremen.

Van Marrewijk, M., & Werre, M. (2003). Multiple levels of corporate sustainability. *Journal of Business Ethics, 44*(2–3), 107–119.

Verhoef, L., & Bossert, M. (2019). *The university campus as a living lab for sustainability: A practitioner's guide and handbook*. Delft, Stuttgart: Delft University of Technology, Hochschule für Technik Stuttgart.

Vogt, M., & Weber, C. (2020). The role of universities in a sustainable society: Why value-free research is neither possible nor desirable. *Sustainability, 12*, 2811. https://doi.org/10.3390/su12072811.

Wals, A. E. J., Walker, K. E., & Corcoran, P. B. (2004). The practice of sustainability in higher education: A synthesis. In P. B. Corcoran & A. E. J. Wals (Eds.), *Higher education and the challenge of sustainability: Problematics, promise, and practice* (Vol. 3, pp. 347–348). Dordrecht, The Netherlands: Springer.

Wilber, K. (2001). *A theory of everything: An integral vision for business, politics, science and spirituality*. Boston: Shambhala.

Wissema, J. G. (2009). *Towards the third generation university: Managing the university in transition*. Cheltenham: Edward Elgar.

World Commission on Environment and Development. (1987). *Our Common Future*. A/42/427. New York. https://sustainabledevelopment.un.org/mil estones/wced. Accessed 25 March 2019.

CHAPTER 6

Facing Gaia in Education: A Storytelling Framework for Teaching Sustainability in Management

Kenneth Mølbjerg Jørgensen

INTRODUCTION

This chapter discusses a storytelling framework for teaching sustainability in management education. The chapter is inspired by Bruno Latour, who in his recent book *Down to Earth* (Latour, 2018) has suggested that climate change now has taken centre stage in the sphere of politics. This implies that sustainability has become an important challenge for management. Management, it is argued, can be regarded as a political process which takes place between stakeholders. Latour argues that what he calls *the Terrestrial*—Earth, Planet, Nature or Gaia—has to be acknowledged as an active agent (Latour, 2018, p. 40) in political processes. The alternative, climate denial, entails a hidden biopolitical narrative that there is not enough space for everybody in this world. Climate denial implies the absence of a common horizon and a world

K. M. Jørgensen (✉)
Department of Urban Studies, Malmö University, Malmö, Sweden
e-mail: kenneth.molbjerg-jorgensen@mau.se

L. Tauginienė and R. Pučėtaitė (eds.), *Managing Social Responsibility in Universities*, https://doi.org/10.1007/978-3-030-70013-3_6

95

in which all humans can prosper equally (Latour, 2018, pp. 1–2). The climate denial, which assumes that there is no limit to growth, thus has no future. We are inevitably facing Gaia (e.g., Latour, 2017) in management and in management education.

Who is Gaia then, and how can we respond to her? For a long time, corporate social responsibility discourse has suggested that companies should balance profit, people, and planet (Vallentin, 2011). Peter McAteer (2019) uses this approach to argue that sustainability is the new advantage. Climate problems are thus turned into a field for economic growth, innovation, and a new Green capitalism. Thus, it is argued that we can respond to Gaia by repairing and extending our existing vocabulary and practices without fundamentally altering our conceptions of what is important in management. Instead this chapter suggests that "facing Gaia", constitutes a fundamental challenge for organizations, management, and for management education. Facing Gaia requires radically rethinking principles for guiding management and organizing in the future. The approach developed in this chapter combines Gaia with storytelling in what is framed as a terrestrial politics in management education.

It is suggested that the combination of Gaia and storytelling implies rediscovering what places mean for stories. It implies understanding how storytelling emerges from places: how landscapes, lakes, streams, hills, forests, and mountains connect with traditions, stories, practices, and identities. Modern life conditions have alienated us from local places in favour of globalization (Escobar, 2008). Gaia storytelling methodology connects organizations with places and are built from those places. Gaia storytelling methodology furthermore celebrates the plurality of life and the unfolding of plural "terrestrials" as principles of ecological, cultural, social, and economic growth.

The chapter offers a methodology of management education which is built from a combination of Gaia and Arendt's notion of storytelling as political action (Arendt, 1998, 2003). The next section discusses Arendt's notion of storytelling as a political appearance among other people. Furthermore, storytelling is discussed in relation to Gaia to identify what Vatter (2006) has called "a politics of natality". This politics connects storytelling with what Arendt (1998) identified as the highest principle of all being, the eternal recurrence of nature's life cycles. However, this principle is substituted with the "Gaia principle" (Lovelock, 1995). A model of the Gaia storytelling organization is then constructed. The last section discusses how management education can be reframed for a terrestrial politics.

Hannah Arendt's Storytelling

Arendt's notion of storytelling is central to the management education framework that is suggested. Her perception of storytelling implies agency. She argues that it is through storytelling that people rework a chronological sequence of events and insert themselves into history (Arendt, 1998; Young-Bruehl, 1977). Thus, storytelling implies allowing actors with a face, unique opinions, feelings, and emotions to speak (Jørgensen, 2020). Through Arendt's notion of storytelling we appeal to the conscious creativity and actions through which "citizens" create and shape stories as responsible and answerable members of communities and societies. The notion of a citizen is consciously chosen here. It implies that before one becomes an organizational subject, one is a citizen of society. This is one of the reasons why we even speak of responsibility and ethics in organizations. Speaking of citizenship is however radical in regard to management and organizations because citizenship implies that we must leave behind one of the most persistent presumptions of management theory, namely, that is performed by single individuals with superior qualities (Spector, 2016; Wilson, 2016).

Instead, management is a practice (Mintzberg, 2004) that people perform together. Thus, abilities to collaborate and the construction of spaces for such politics are important managerial skills and competencies. Arendt's notion of storytelling is important here for constructing such an understanding of management. Her understanding of storytelling is also different from dominant understandings of organizational storytelling. Storytelling is often used to understand meaning and identity work in relation to changing circumstances (Humphreys & Brown, 2002). Identity is understood as expressed in self-narratives which mirror reflexive dialogues that a person has with himself or herself (Brown & Coupland, 2015). Such narratives are seen as shaped within power relations and as the effects of power relations (Riach, Rumens, & Tyler, 2016). Arendt's perception of storytelling breaks with these understandings in several ways:

1. Stories break with power relations in the sense that true stories always contain a new beginning. Accounts that only represent power or discourses are not stories, because they do not reflect the actor's creative and reflected intentions but instead repeat ritualized norms and traditions (Totschnig, 2017).

2. Stories occur in the spaces between people. To tell a story implies appearing before others and disclosing one's intentions, interests, and motivations (Arendt, 1998). This also implies that storytelling is a political concept. This does not suggest that narrative identity work is not important. It is very important that stories are reflexive. On the other hand, stories have no political significance if they are not shared with others (Arendt, 2003).

3. To be able to tell stories in order to touch others and to be confirmed as an actor with an opinion that counts as valuable and meaningful in the community is an existential condition (Jackson, 2013). This means that there has to be consistency between how actors appear in the political play between people and the actor's intentions, motives, and interests.

Adopting Arendt's notion of storytelling implies operating with a clear distinction between organizational discourse and stories. Discourse is usually understood as setting a frame for what can be legitimately said and done (Agamben, 1999; Butler, 2015). This space can be more or less broad or narrow. The boundaries between what cannot and what can be said are furthermore not necessarily clear. These boundaries can be very diffuse and are always subject for negotiation and struggle. Stories are always beyond discourse in the sense that a story, in order to be a story, must reflect the actor's intentions. Thus, the rework of the sequence of events into a story reflects the actor's agency. It is through stories that the actor steps forwards. She does not represent power even if she has to use language and discourse to put a new story together. To speak and to tell stories requires an actor with intentions and interests. A story loses its vitality and creativity if this actor is not present (Birmingham, 2002).

This also suggest that stories, according to Arendt, cannot be mistaken for self-narratives. These are constructed in the activity that Arendt refers to as thinking and are results of deep two-in-one dialogue that people have with themselves or a friend (Arendt, 2003). Thinking is important for free and reflexive speech. Basically, however, storytelling is about something else. It is about appearing before others in a public space. In such spaces, people transform our experiences to make them fit for public appearance (Arendt, 1998). The term "public" has two meanings. It means that peoples' stories can be seen, heard, and responded to by others in a public space. Second, the term "public" implies having something in common, which is different from our private spaces (Arendt,

1998). This is obviously important for management. Managers have to make their intentions public in order to manage. They have to do so in front of the organization's stakeholders. In short, it can be claimed that the unfolding of management takes place in formal or spontaneously emerging public spaces. In those spaces, managers disclose their opinions, intentions and values and make them subject to visibility, dialogue, conversation, and recognition but also to criticism and resistance.

In appearances, a problematic play occurs between individual and organizational interests. However, it is in such appearances that managers become managers. Such moments constitute the moment of truth in management because it is in such spaces that managers touch others as well as they are touched by those others (e.g., Jackson, 2013). Appearances before others are decisive for organizational change and can serve different interests. Appearances can contain questions of legitimacy or can seek to mobilize resources in relation to desired changes. At the same time, there is an important play which is decisive for the potential for learning and creativity among the partners. This play consists of managers recognizing that appearances happen in front of other people who also have a need of being seen, heard, and validated as actors with opinions that matter. Without such appearances, such spaces will not contain the sensitivity and vulnerability that is necessary for learning, transformation, and collective action.

Arendt calls the purest of such public spaces "a space of appearance" (1998). It is a space in which people as citizens can exchange experiences and opinions freely. Such a space never exists but always has to be created by the actors who are present. It always exists as a potential wherever people are together. A space of appearance cannot be designed by third parties, but spaces can be created, which, through breaking with everyday rituals and power distributions, can promote other and freer ways of expressing and exchanging stories.

Appearance is, as a final point, an existential condition. Storytelling is not only about creation of meaning or learning for that matter. It is also a question of being recognized and validated as an actor, who counts. Thus, it is necessary for our identity that we are recognized as members of societies, communities, and organizations (Jackson, 2013). Therefore, such dialogical spaces are important for organizational wellbeing. If managers and organizations do not create them, they emerge as separate spaces, which metaphorically can be described as "a politics of the street" (Butler, 2015). Such a second life exists in all organizations. But it is a necessity for the coherence of the organization that there is a connection between such grounded politics and the organization's strategies.

Common spaces, where people can meet and talk across differences, are necessary in organizations. Jackson (2013, p. 49) argues that what is taking place in those spaces, is a question of "emplacement" rather than "emplotment". This is important because the latter has dominated narrative research (Boje, 2001; Jørgensen & Boje, 2010; Ricœur, 1984). Emplacement, however, captures the need for belonging and for being rooted among others in a community and, as it is argued later, in nature (Jørgensen, 2020). The opposite is of course to be "displaced", which, on the one hand, is a feeling of marginalization, alienation, and powerlessness and, on the other hand, is to be out-of-place in being non-grounded in nature's life cycles.

FACING GAIA

Hannah Arendt argued that what is embedded in storytelling is the human condition of natality—rebirth. To be able to tell and share stories implies having an agency in one's life, which implies that people can begin again. This new beginning is the rebirth she associates with action. It implies that human life is not just about being able to survive in a physical sense but to be able to have a control and agency in one's own life and to be able to act politically. It is therefore that true stories, as mentioned above, always contain an element of a new beginning. Arendt thus perceived storytelling as the only true political action (Tassinari, Piredda, & Bertolotti, 2017). Such political action requires the presence of others and thus always takes place between people who validate such beginnings as important and meaningful. It is important that management students become prepared for such a politics of natality, which implies being able to communicate, collaborate and interact with others in order to enable collective action.

Central themes in management can be organized using storytelling as "appearance". Strategies, for instance, can be analyzed as stories in which organizations step forward and appear before their stakeholders for the purpose of gaining legitimacy and support for its desired course of action. Strategy, understood as the organization's story of itself, is constituted by this double play where the organization, on the one hand, tries to create a story and identity for itself; on the other hand, this identity is also decided by what the internal and external stakeholders allow this identity to become. Managers face the same double play. They rely on appearing before others and making their intentions public before these others. Management is thus decided by the political play between actors. Power, dominance, and suppression of voices are parts of this play. This suggests that inclusion and exclusion of voices are inherent to any organizational process.

So far, the voices of earth and climate have not played a huge role in organizational relationships or in management but have been marginalized. Instead, politics has been understood as a play between people. But there is always a background, or rather a "ground", on which such collective action takes place and without which collective politics among people would be meaningless (Serres, 1995). The Paris Agreement and the adoption of the 17 sustainable development goals (SDGs) reflects a new situation in which the climate question, understood in a broad sense as the relations between human beings and the material conditions of the life (Latour, 2018), has taken centre stage in politics.

The climate crisis poses new questions for ethics and management. Arendt's storytelling as the rebirth of ourselves in action is an entry point. She argued that this human condition was submitted to what she called the highest principle of all being, namely, the eternal recurrence of nature's life cycles (Arendt, 1998). Vatter (2006) suggests in this connection that Arendt's ethical position can be captured in a politics of natality where the memory of being born from a plurality of species and life-forms is always embedded in an unconditional love for the world in all its variations. Totschnig (2017) argues however that for Arendt, it is only human beings who have the capacity of beginning again. Arendt's notion of nature reflects the limited Western understanding of this nature, when Arendt was writing in the 1950s and 1960s. Her perception of nature is that it would run around in circles and endlessly repeats itself if it was not for humans acting into-nature.

Latour's Gaia is different here. It is inspired by James Lovelock's (1995) Gaia hypothesis that Earth is living and self-regulating. Latour emphasizes that Gaia is not the Globe (Latour, 2016) but instead puts our attention towards the local and highly differentiated and multiple eco-systems that are living and breathing in what he and his colleagues call *the critical zone* (Arènes, Latour, & Gaillardet, 2018). This critical zone is a thin layer of topsoil that lies on the surface of the earth. It is in this layer that matter has shaped and modified life, and it is here that life is unfolding and changing in multiple ways. We humans are part of this thin skin enfolded upon the surface of the earth. Arènes et al. (2018) suggest that life moves in cycles, not in circles. This means that life is both repetitive and changing as the cycles of life become entangled with other life cycles. Thus, it is not that the climate is changing, which is dangerous. It is the acceleration and speed with which it changes, which are dangerous and unpredictable. Latour thus argues that Gaia can turn into a monster because of us (Latour, 2011). Furthermore, it is naïve to think that we can control Gaia. She has an agency of her own.

Importantly also, every place has its own critical zone. For Latour, place becomes much more important. Places are not only important in a physical sense. Entangled with place are particular flora and fauna but also cultural traditions and practices. A poem by Jaime Rivas (quoted in Escobar, 2008, p. 27. Translated by John C. Chasteen) illustrates the point.

> This land is ours
> Here we've been trees and birds
> And learned the rhythm of the waves
> And become children of the water...
> This land is ours
> As is the happiness
> We've invented

> This land is ours
> We founded it with pain and blood
> It is the bed of our free dreams
> The cradle of our desires
> And the tomb of our elders
> The water here tastes like us

This poem illustrates the meaning of identities, stories, and pride that are tied to places and make no sense outside these places. We are of-the-world and thus of place (Barad, 2007). Places are in our blood. We are made from the water, the air, and the soil in these places. The critical zone puts our attention towards these local places and the multiple variations of lifeforms and matter that make up these places. Place entails a socio-material-ecological approach rather than a technological approach to the climate question. Facing Gaia in management education is facing the importance of place: landscapes, rivers, flora, fauna, mountains, glaciers, fields, mud, and soil as well as practices, songs, identities, traditions, people, etc. We are embodied places (De Certeau, 1984; Jørgensen & Strand, 2014) and exist in a state of dependence on the plurality of life that exists in places. In this connection, Latour suggests a radical move which he captures in the idea of the Terrestrial as a new dominant political agent (Latour, 2018). Importantly, the Terrestrial implies the multiplication of agencies as well as dissolving the duality between human and non-human agents (De Freitas, 2020; Gleason, 2019). We humans are terrestrials along with many other species. It is this relationship between Gaia and the Terrestrial that we need to integrate into management and management education.

Gaia and the Sustainable Development Goals

The entanglement of Gaia and the Terrestrial requires us to rethink how we relate to sustainability in a physical sense and how we relate to others and organize in a social sense. Rockström and Sukhdev (2016) have reorganized the UN Sustainable Development Goals (SDGs) in ways in which they come close to the terrestrial management education approach that I suggest and in which storytelling is central. They argue that the biosphere goals: "Clean water and sanitation", "Climate action", "Life on land" and "Life in the water" constitute the foundation on which we have to build societies and organizations. The societal level is the second level. This can be captured through Arendt's dictum of *the right to have rights* (DeGooyer, Hunt, Maxwell, & Moyn, 2018). The right to have rights includes more than membership in a society and rights to vote but also rights like access to education, food, healthcare, and transportation. Such rights supplement biosphere rights like access to clean water, clean air, and a living and breathing diverse nature. Access to such rights is necessary to be included as full citizens of a society. Organizations play an important role here in creating the conditions for healthy and attractive jobs, gender equality, and for decent economic conditions. The economic level is based on a healthy biosphere and a healthy society. Importantly, it gives a contrasting image of a company's responsibility than, for instance, the corporate social responsibility pyramid which is founded upon economy and law (Carroll, 2016).

If we read the SDG pyramid through the lenses of Gaia and the terrestrial, organizations have a far wider responsibility towards local eco-systems, biodiversity, and water quality. Thus, responsibility towards climate cannot be reduced to lowering CO_2 emissions, but it is much more detailed and local. Furthermore, responsibility is also a matter of human resource management policies and practices, e.g., inclusion of minorities, gender equality, decent jobs, and work conditions, and so forth. Importantly, it is part of managerial responsibilities to perceive and treat organizational subjects as citizens who have a right to participate. Participation is a precondition for assuming responsibility. Participation is built into the very idea of storytelling and the space of appearance and the idea that management is a collective practice done in collaboration between people. In Fig. 6.1, I have built a management model based on the idea that management as the right kind of politics are submitted to Gaia's life cycles and to the plurality of people, cultures, and social practices. The politics of natality must become embedded in three activities that correspond to Arendt's distinction between labour, work, and action. In the model, they are translated as economy, technology, and politics.

The model collects the different dimensions that I have discussed above. It provides inputs for what management education needs to address for facing Gaia. In the next sections, I will discuss how to translate this place-based approach to management education.

Fig. 6.1 Management as the right kind of politics

Universities as a Cradle for Terrestrial Management

Albert Einstein once said that "we cannot solve our problems with the same thinking we used when we created them" (see https://www.pinter est.com/pin/179018153909676250/). In the context of this chapter, it entails throwing away much of the economic logic that has dominated managerial thinking since its dawn. Managerialism is associated with rise of economics and capitalism as dominant discourses. With economics came unlimited growth, expansionism, colonialism, and imperialism as the hallmarks of human endeavour and happiness. Benjamin (Arendt, 1999; Benjamin, 1999; Demiryol, 2018), on the other hand, associated capitalism with endless destruction of nature, culture, society, and tradition. Instead of beauty and progress, he saw rubbish, trash and wreckage piling up in the trail of economic development.

Sustainability implies rethinking management education. This implies also rethinking the institutions, universities, and business schools that host management education. Gaia and the Terrestrial are helpful here. A terrestrial management education is built on a philosophy of place that integrates nature, culture, and society as a foundational element. The principle of the Terrestrial is the appearance and development of a natural, cultural, and social life that unfolds in plural ways arounds us, within us, and beneath us. This principle is non-negotiable. Rich varieties of terrestrial life imply rich cultural, social, and economic life, as far as this is linked to citizenship, inclusion, gender equality, education, healthcare, and decent jobs.

Such thinking is also beyond the requirements for scientific evidence and justification. We need to do it simply because it is the right thing to do. Management science has never shown any understanding or sympathy for Gaia anyway. We need to have courage and we need to be guided by what Che Guevara, according to Sandoval (2013), said was the guiding principle of the revolution, namely "love". In Fig. 6.2, I sketch seven principles for terrestrial management education that integrate the principles of dependency and plurality of life with human technological practices as well as with collective action understood as storytelling and story-making. These seven principles are not to be understood as following a particular sequence or a circle. They are more thought of as interdependent cycles that are entangled and condition each other.

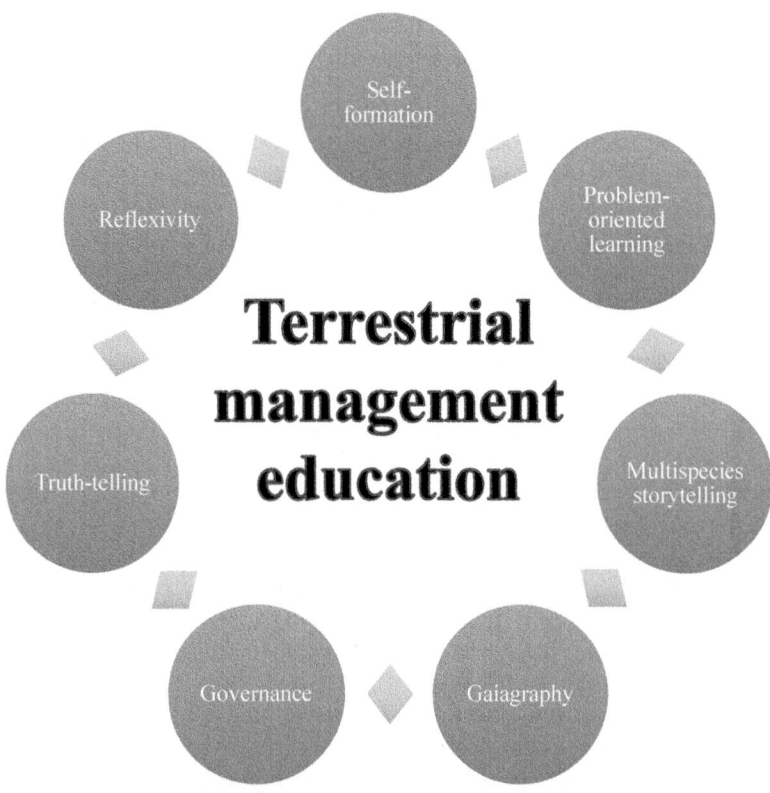

Fig. 6.2 Terrestrial management education

STORYTELLING IS SELF-FORMATION

This storytelling principle incorporates the principles of action and uniqueness as integral parts of management education. Instead of standardized curricula, this principle emphasizes the construction of spaces in which management students can express and shape themselves as unique persons. Management education is thus a project that integrates the need for meeting academic standards with a unique storytelling capability. Storytelling implies that participatory practices replace the lecture, dialogues replace monologues, thinking replaces repetition (Freire, 2017), experimentation and play replace formal learning goals

(Strand, 2012), and writing becomes a matter of creative thinking and agency instead of reproducing discourse.

Storytelling is furthermore important because it entails being created from place and territory. Our stories are empty without places, traditions, cultures, and practices. Stories have a time, a place, and a mind (Boje, 2001). Management students' stories are thus the starting point for internalizing and personalizing the theories and concepts of management education. It is important that management education becomes a space of appearance for students in which they can work with participating in a political way in organizations and society from their identities as shaped by place and space. Facing Gaia entails incorporating the voices of water, air, animals, plants, forests, and landscapes as well as gender, equality, and citizenship into management education. Self-formation entails self-directed learning and participation and learning spaces, and it is an integral part of problem-based learning (see below). In continuing management education, auto-biographical and ethnographic storytelling methods (Jørgensen, 2018; Spry, 2016) can be used for having managers writing and reflecting about themselves as managers.

Storytelling Is Directed Towards Practical Problems

Problem-oriented learning is a methodology for locating management education and learning at the intersection between universities, communities, and societies. Practical problems are the sites for value conflicts, differences of opinion, intentions, and stakes (Dewey, 2004). Students' stories have to engage with such problems or phenomena in order to be integrated with the world. Freire (2017) has argued that a critical emancipatory idea of education is merged with societal issues in problem-oriented learning (e.g., Jørgensen, Strand, & Thomassen, 2012). Through problem-oriented projects, students become engaged in collaboration with external stakeholders in terms of how they, for example, struggle with the climate crisis. Furthermore, problem-oriented learning is a natural solution for making education partners in a new collaborative model between four sectors in society: business, the public sector, civil society, and education. Such collaboration is seen as important for organizing society in relation to grand challenges that the SDGs are responses to (Bason, 2018).

The Aalborg model for problem-based learning (Kolmos & Fink, 2004) has institutionalized the learning method in problem-oriented project groups which work with concrete practical problems for at least half of the time in each semester. Apart from working in the intersection between theory and practice, problem-oriented learning is a site for collaboration and dialogue between people. Such learning models can be expanded according to the principle of the Terrestrial through exploring and mapping complex relations between organizational practices and the climate in order to situate organizations as a companion to the life of Gaia (Jørgensen & Boje, 2020). The project is thus a site for experimentation with new solutions and practices in which ideas and concepts can be exchanged between education, businesses, organizations, and institutions.

Multispecies Storytelling

The notion of the Terrestrial implies distributing agency to human and non-humans alike in a way in which the duality between human and non-agencies are dissolved (Jørgensen, Strand, Hayden, Larsen, & Sparre, 2020). Instead we are terrestrials who exist in companionship and dependency with many other terrestrials (Gleason, 2019). Haraway calls it multispecies storytelling which is when "… multispecies players, who are enmeshed in partial and flawed translations across differences, redo ways of living and dying attuned to still possible finite flourishing, still possible recuperation" (Haraway, 2016, p. 10). In others, organizations must be transformed into partners and companions for terrestrial flourishing and recovery.

Multispecies storytelling implies for education to contribute to the appearance, unfolding, and flourishing of the plurality of life itself. In other words, business and management decisions have to be made on the basis of caretaking and the growth of natural and cultural resources. It is only from this understanding that businesses and organizations can harvest the fruits of nature. For example, it means that the circular economy, understood as the collection and recycling of waste, can play only a minor role compared to what a more deliberate focus on reducing the consumption of resources in management can do for the rebirth of terrestrial living. For management education, this implies a focus on the biosphere goals (see Fig. 6.1) as a basis for the organization's life cycles: product life cycles, financial cycles, supply chain cycles, transportation, waste management, and recycling as well as care for what the substances that are being used in production processes do for the possibilities of multispecies storytelling.

STORYTELLING MAPS GAIAGRAPHIES

Latour and colleagues (Arènes et al., 2018) use the term gaiagraphy as a way of mapping the entangled life cycles of the critical zone that make up the local places in which terrestrials co-exist in companionship with one another. Gaiagraphy is thus a critical part for organizations to imagine and monitor its effects on the vital processes of the critical zone: water, air, bio-diversity, life-on-land, life-in-the water, landscapes, soil, sand etc. This kind of mapping may involve the collaboration with experts hired in municipalities or state institutions, but it also involves the stories and practical experiences of people on the ground. In a Gaiagraphy, Gaia takes the central stage as the new dominant political voice.

For organizations, this implies understanding how it is part of life cycles that recur and change with different velocities and intensities. Gaiagraphy implies making the world "flat" (Arènes et al., 2018; Jørgensen et al., 2020) in the metaphorical sense that we have to understand how the life cycles of the world recur all round us and through our actions. Material storytelling, artefacts, and sand-trays (Strand, 2012) can, for example, be used to create three-dimensional miniature models in which managers and students can imagine relations and consequences on grander scale. In this way, it is possible to ground the multi-voiced dialogues necessary for management education and learning (Bager, 2015). Such methods are parts of finding ways to map how organizations and managers affect nature in order to understand, on a larger and local scale, how we are part of and affect nature through organizational actions. Far from being a restrictive position, however, such care-giving and care-taking celebrate life itself and help develop organizations into much more desirable and happy places to live and work in.

STORYTELLING IS DIRECTED TOWARDS GOVERNANCE

The fifth principle of terrestrial management education is governance. Could Gaia be the one who could finally tear down the silos between institutions and organizations in society and make us realize that we need to collaborate across professional and institutional boundaries and differences in order to find effective solutions that benefit us all. According to the principle of governance, management is not only an interorganizational but also an interdisciplinary practice between businesses people, public administrators, politicians, artists, artisans, activists, biologists, geologists, physicists, communication experts, and engineers as well as other professions. Management has been confused with measurement and has embarrassed itself greatly in that process. Management instead is a practice (Mintzberg, 2004) and takes place in the between.

At Malmö University in Sweden, a new education program has been established that focuses on management at the intersection between business, public organizations, and civil society, including non-profit organizations. Management is thus seen as part of societal development, and the program is located at the Department of Urban Development at the Faculty of Culture and Society. This signals the strong interdisciplinary and intersectional focus of the department, where the goal is to combine different professional perspectives into a management education program. Teachers in the program come from urban development, computer science, education, and public governance as well as from management and business studies. The purpose is that management students become able to embrace diversity and different professional perspectives and can work at the intersection between different sectors.

STORYTELLING IS TRUTH-TELLING

Storytelling as appearance implies that storytelling is also truth-telling. As noted previously, storytelling is to appear before others with one's own voice, intentions, and interests. This requires integration with and validation from other voices including Gaia, other terrestrials, communities, and organizations. Truth-telling is a precondition for the emergence of a space of appearance in which we are *together with* others and neither for nor against them as noted by Arendt (1998, p. 180). From Foucault's work on parrhesia, Maria Tamboukou (2012) has identified four essential themes of truth-telling. First, speaking the truth has to do with "unhiddenness" and has nothing to do with assertion or correspondence. Management thus implies honesty and frankness and is thus associated with creating conditions of trust among people. If there is not some honesty and frankness, it is difficult to imagine organizations as a common space. Second, truth-telling implies speaking the truth even when there is risk or danger for the truth-teller. Management seen as initiating new beginnings is risky, but it is also by such risk-taking that managers become managers instead of representatives of power. Sustainable management requires people who are willing and able to run the risk. Otherwise, there will be no new thing under the sun (e.g., Arendt, 1998).

Third, truth-telling is a form of criticism towards oneself and another, and it should always be told from marginalized voices' points of view. In the case of the terrestrial, the marginalized voices constitute the voices of non-human terrestrials, Gaia as well as the people living in precarious conditions, who suffer and are most exposed to climate changes. Fourth, the telling of truth is regarded as a duty and is further related to freedom. Freedom does not entail being able to talk and act freely and independently of everything and everybody. Freedom entails being answerable and responsible for Gaia, people, communities, and societies. For both the truthteller and the addressees, there is a lot at stake in truth-telling. In order to work, a kind of "parrhesiastic pact" is required in which participants also have an obligation to demonstrate their greatness by accepting to be told the truth. For example, truth-telling can be fostered in management through communication training and appearing before others. We have also experimented with using material artefacts, cubes with the SDGs, pictures, posters, and paintings. These are means for imagining and constructing different stories. In truth-telling sessions, students have to dare something in order to make them work. But, on the other hand, this is what management and learning is about. Finally, truth-telling, as a critical storytelling, can be fostered through working with problems of the marginalized or excluded. This involves working with gender equality, racial equality, community development, etc. (i.e., projects where students are challenged because they work with people radically different from themselves).

Storytelling Requires Reflexive Practices

Finally, storytelling requires the reflexive practices, which Arendt referred to as deep two-in-one dialogues with the self (Arendt, 2003). Such practices of deep thinking are important for becoming a subject. Unlike relational reflexivity (Cunliffe & Eriksen, 2011) or reflexive dialogical practices (Cunliffe, 2002), reflexivity is a personal practice and a deep mode of contemplation in which persons make up their minds about ethical and moral standards for being in the world. Such reflexive practices require a private space that is undisturbed by the presence of others. Such practices are inevitably disturbed when one interacts with others. Therefore, it is necessary that such practices take place in solitude or, alternatively, when a person is engaged in deep conversations with a friend (Arendt, 1998). The distinction between a private and public space is thus important for Arendt and entails the construction and respect of spaces, which are private. This is important in times in which organizations as well as education have become more and more interested in the private sphere of organizational subjects. Ole Fogh Kirkeby and colleagues have developed the protreptic method (Kirkeby, Hede, Mejlhede, & Larsen, 2008) with the special purpose that continuing management can explore deep values such as what is true, what is just, what is beautiful, etc.

Conclusions

Sustainability requires radically rethinking management education. This chapter has proposed such rethinking through the notions of Gaia, the Terrestrial, and storytelling. Terrestrial politics implies that the configuration of place becomes much more important in storytelling. The chapter has argued for seven storytelling moves that need to be dominant and integrated with sustainable management education: self-formation, practical problems, multispecies storytelling, gaiagraphy, governance, truthtelling, and reflexive practices. I perceive these storytelling cycles as constituting a living ethics of life instead of an ethics of restraint. We have a long way to go towards a terrestrial management education. These seven storytelling cycles can help us guide the way.

References

Agamben, G. (1999). *Remnants of Auschwitz: The witness and the archive.* Cambridge, MA: Zone Books.

Arendt, H. (1998). *The human condition* (2nd ed.). Chicago: University of Chicago Press.

Arendt, H. (1999). Introduction: Walter Benjamin: 1892–1940. In W. Benjamin (Ed.), *Illuminations* (pp. 7–58). Bournemouth: Pimlico.

Arendt, H. (2003). *Responsibility and judgment.* New York: Schocken Books.

Arènes, A., Latour, B., & Gaillardet, J. (2018). Giving depth to the surface: An exercise in the Gaia-graphy of critical zones. *The Anthropocene Review, 5*(2), 120–135. https://doi.org/10.1177/2053019618782257.

Bager, A. (2015). *Theorising and analysing plurivocality and dialogue in organizational and leadership development practices: Discussion and discourse analysis of dialogic practices in a leadership development forum.* Aalborg: Aalborg Universitetsforlag. https://doi.org/10.5278/vbn.phd.hum.00023.

Barad, K. (2007). *Meeting the Universe Halfway: Quantum physics and the entanglement of matter and meaning*. Durham, NC: Duke University Press.

Bason, C. (2018). *Leading public sector innovation: Co-creating for a better society*. Bristol, UK; Portland, OR, USA: Bristol University Press. https://doi.org/10.2307/j.ctt9qgnsd.

Benjamin, W. (1999). The storyteller—Reflections on the work of Nicolai Leskov. In H. Arendt (Ed.), *Illuminations* (pp. 83–107). Bournemouth: Pimlico.

Birmingham, P. (2002). Heidegger and Arendt: The birth of political action and speech. In F. Raffoul & D. Pettigrew (Eds.), *Heidegger and practical philosophy* (pp. 191–204). Albany, NY: State University of New York Press.

Boje, D. M. (2001). *Narrative methods for organizational & communication research*. London: Sage.

Brown, A. D., & Coupland, C. (2015). Identity threats, identity work and elite professionals. *Organization Studies, 36*(10), 1315–1336. https://doi.org/10.1177/0170840615593594.

Butler, J. (2015). *Notes toward a performative theory of assembly*. Harvard University Press.

Carroll, A. B. (2016). Carroll's pyramid of CSR: Taking another look. *International Journal of Corporate Social Responsibility, 1*(3), 1–8.

Cunliffe, A. L. (2002). Reflexive dialogical practice in management learning. *Management Learning, 33*(1), 35–61.

Cunliffe, A. L., & Eriksen, M. (2011). Relational leadership. *Human Relations, 64*(11), 1425–1449. https://doi.org/10.1177/0018726711418388.

De Certeau, M. (1984). *The practice of everyday life*. Oakland, CA: University of California Press.

De Freitas, E. (2020). Science studies and the metamorphic multiple earth: Bruno Latour's risky diplomacy. *Cultural Studies—Critical Methodologies, 20*(3), 203–2012.

DeGooyer, S., Hunt, A., Maxwell, L., & Moyn, S. (2018). *The right to have rights*. London: Verso.

Demiryol, G. I. (2018). Arendt and Benjamin: Tradition, progress and break with the past. *Journal of the Philosophy of History, 12*, 142–163.

Dewey, J. (2004). *Democracy and education*. North Chelmsford, MA: Courier Corporation.

Escobar, A. (2008). *Territories of difference: Place, movements, life, redes*. Durham, NC: Duke University Press.

Freire, P. (2017). *Pedagogy of the oppressed*. London: Penguin Books.

Gleason, T. (2019). Towards a terrestrial education: A commentary on Bruno Latour's down to earth. *Environmental Education Research, 25*(6), 977–986.

Haraway, D. J. (2016). *Staying with the trouble: Making Kin in the Chthulucene*. Durham, NC: Duke University Press.

Humphreys, M., & Brown, A. D. (2002). Narratives of organizational identity and identification: A case study of hegemony and resistance. *Organization Studies, 23*(3), 421–447.

Jackson, M. (2013). *The politics of storytelling: Variations on a theme by Hannah Arendt*. Copenhagen: Museum Tusculanum Press.

Jørgensen, K. M. (2018). The politics of space: An Arendtian framework for leadership development. *Revista Cuadernos de Administracion, 31*(57), 105–128. http://dx.doi.org/10.11444/Javeriana.cao.31-57.tpsa.

Jørgensen, K. M. (2020). Storytelling, space and power: An Arendtian account of subjectivity in organizations. *Organization*. https://doi.org/10.1177/135 0508420928522.

Jørgensen, K. M., & Boje, D. M. (2010). Resituating narrative and story in business ethics. *Business Ethics: A European Review, 19*(3), 253–264. https://doi.org/10.1111/j.1467-8608.2010.01593.x.

Jørgensen, K. M., & Boje, D. M. (2020). Storytelling sustainability in problem-based learning. In R. V. Turcan & J. E. Reilly (Eds.), *Populism in higher education curriculum development*. London: Palgrave Macmillan.

Jørgensen, K. M., & Strand, A. M. C. (2014). Material storytelling—Learning as intra-active becoming. In K. M. Jørgensen & C. Largarcha-Martinez (Eds.), *Critical narrative inquiry—Storytelling, sustainability and power* (pp. 53–72). New York: Nova Science Publishers.

Jørgensen, K. M., Strand, A. M. C., & Thomassen, A. O. (2012). Conceptual bases of problem-based learning. In J. E. Groccia, M. A. T. Alsudairy, & W. Buskist (Eds.), *Handbook of college and university teaching: A global perspective* (pp. 440–456). London: Sage.

Jørgensen, K. M., Strand, A. M. C., Hayden, J., Larsen, J., & Sparre, M. (2020). *Gaia storytelling and the learning organization*. Paper presented at The Quantum Storytelling Conference, New Mexico, 16–19 December, 2020.

Kirkeby, O. F., Hede, T. D., Mejlhede, M., & Larsen, J. (2008). *Protreptik—Filosofisk coaching i ledelse*. Samfundslitteratur.

Kolmos, A., & Fink, F. K. (2004). *The Aalborg PBL model—Progress, diversity and challenges*. Aalborg: Aalborg University Press.

Latour, B. (2011). *Waiting for Gaia: Composing the common world through arts and politics—A lecture at the French Institute*. http://www.bruno-latour.fr/sites/default/files/124-GAIA-LONDON-SPEAP_0.pdf. Accessed 11 January 2020.

Latour, B. (2016, June 2). *Bruno Latour: Why Gaia is not the globe*. https://www.youtube.com/watch?v=7AGg-oHzPsM. Accessed 2 October 2020.

Latour, B. (2017). *Facing Gaia: Eight lectures on the new climatic regime*. Hoboken, NJ: Wiley.

Latour, B. (2018). *Down to earth: Politics in the new climatic regime*. Cambridge, UK: Polity.

Lovelock, J. (1995). *Gaia—A new look at life on earth*. Oxford: Oxford University Press.

McAteer, P. (2019). *Sustainability is the new advantage—Leadership, change and the future of business*. London: Anthem Press.

Mintzberg, H. (2004). *Managers, not MBAs: A hard look at the soft practice of managing and management development*. Oakland, CA: Berrett-Koehler Publishers.

Riach, K., Rumens, N., & Tyler, M. (2016). Towards a Butlerian methodology: Undoing organizational performativity through anti-narrative research. *Human Relations, 69*(11), 2069–2089. https://doi.org/10.1177/001872 6716632050.

Ricœur, P. (1984). *Time and narrative*. Chicago: University of Chicago Press.

Rockström, J., & Sukhdev, P. (2016). *How food connects all the SDGs*. Stockholm Resilience Center. https://www.stockholmresilience.org/research/research-news/2016-06-14-how-food-connects-all-the-sdgs.html. Accessed 20 September 2020.

Sandoval, C. (2013). *Methodology of the oppressed*. Minneapolis, MN: University of Minnesota Press.

Serres, M. (1995). *The natural contract*. An Arbor, MI: University of Michigan Press.

Spector, B. (2016). *Discourse on leadership: A critical appraisal*. Cambridge, UK: Cambridge University Press.

Spry, T. (2016). *Autoethnography and the other: Unsettling power through Utopian performatives*. Routledge.

Strand, A. M. C. (2012). *Enacting the between: On dis/continuous intra-active becoming of/through an apparatus of material storytelling. Book 1: Posing (an apparatus of) material storytelling as discontinuous intra-active rework of organizational practices*. https://vbn.aau.dk/en/publications/enacting-the-between-on-discontinuous-intra-active-becoming-ofthr. Accessed 27 March 2020.

Tamboukou, M. (2012). Truth telling in Foucault and Arendt: Parrhesia, the pariah and academics in dark times. *Journal of Education Policy, 27*(6), 849–865.

Tassinari, V., Piredda, F., & Bertolotti, E. (2017). Storytelling in design for social innovation and politics: A reading through the lenses of Hannah Arendt. *The Design Journal, 20*(sup1), S3486–S3495. https://doi.org/10.1080/146 06925.2017.1352852.

Totschnig, W. (2017). Arendt's notion of natality—An attempt of clarification. *Ideas y Valores, 66*(165), 327–346. http://dx.doi.org/10.15446/ideasyval ores.v66n165.55202.

Vallentin, S. (2011). *Afkastet og anstændigheden*. Frederiksberg: Samfundslitteratur.

Vatter, M. (2006). Natality and biopolitics in Hannah Arendt. *Revista de Ciencia Política, 26*(2), 137–159.

Wilson, S. (2016). *Thinking differently about leadership: A critical history of leadership studies*. Northampton, MA: Edward Elgar.

Young-Bruehl, E. (1977). Hannah Arendt's storytelling. *Social Research, 44*(1), 183–190. JSTOR. https://www.jstor.org/stable/40970279. Accessed 23 February 2020.

CHAPTER 7

Higher Education Teachers' Perspectives on Inputs, Processes, and Outputs of Teaching Service-Learning Courses

Katharina Resch and Gabriel Dima

INTRODUCTION

University Social Responsibility (USR) has been discussed on various levels, connected to the first, second, or third mission of higher education institutions—research, teaching, and its Third Sector activities (Menezes, Coelho, & Amorim, 2018). In this chapter, we focus on a promising and innovative teaching approach, 'Service-Learning' (Aramburuzabala, McIlrath, & Opazo, 2019; Rutti, LaBonte, Helms, Hervani, & Sarkarat, 2016), which connects the second and third mission of universities in

K. Resch (✉)
Center for Teacher Education and Faculty of Educational Science,
University of Vienna, Vienna, Austria
e-mail: katharina.resch@univie.ac.at

G. Dima
Department of Electronics, Telecommunications and IT, University Politehnica of Bucharest, Bucharest, Romania
e-mail: gabriel.dima@upb.ro

L. Tauginienė and R. Pučėtaitė (eds.), *Managing Social Responsibility in Universities*, https://doi.org/10.1007/978-3-030-70013-3_7

117

a unique way and thus promotes social responsibility. In this form of applied coursework teaching connects theory and practice by allowing students to participate in a service that meets community needs and to reflect on the experience in class and to gain an enhanced sense of civic engagement (Bringle, Hatcher, & McIntosh, 2006; Furco, 2009). In higher education, keeping didactic competences up to date is a challenge for teachers in all disciplines and applied coursework meeting real needs of community partners might be viewed as more challenging than teaching in other formats. Why some teachers prefer teaching these courses and others do not, remains open to date. Teachers might choose to update their skills in their field of study and prioritize subject-teaching, rather than generic, methodological and didactic skills. Furthermore, teachers in higher education, who are used to teaching theory courses, might disregard providing guidance to students in an applied coursework setting, such as in Service-Learning. Service-Learning is a pedagogy that connects academic learning and a community service experience (Furco, 2009), and thus contains both 'service' and 'learning'. Service-Learning as a methodology is unknown to many teachers, although they teach subjects in which the methodology would add value. Service-Learning can include Third Sector services in schools, social initiatives, public institutions, or non-for-profit organizations (Waldstein & Reiher, 2001). In many disciplines, connecting theory and practice is a major challenge for higher education teachers, such as medicine or teacher education (Tatebe, 2013). "Connecting theory and practice through both the design of thoughtful coursework and the integration of high-quality (...) work in settings where good practice is supported" (Darling-Hammond, 2017), is currently named as one of the main challenges in higher education. Service-Learning is considered as a practice between the higher education institution, the teacher, faculty, students, and community partners—bringing about benefits for all sides, connecting theory and practice and enhancing social responsibility of students (Rutti et al., 2016). However, in this chapter we want to focus on the perspective of the teacher, since teachers' perspectives are "relatively invisible in the discourse of service learning" (Boland, 2014, p. 183), but highly relevant in professionally guiding students to deliver both the 'service' and the 'learning' components in Service-Learning.

Especially in English-speaking higher education systems, Service-Learning has a long tradition since it started to develop as a pedagogy in the 1980s during initiatives like Campus Compact (1985) or Campus

Outreach Opportunity League (1984). Currently, and in connection with the idea of strengthening Third Sector activities a discussion about the implementation of Service-Learning as an innovative pedagogy in higher education has entered the European higher education sector more and more. Ireland, Spain, and Germany have pioneer positions in Europe when it comes to Service-Learning policies, national networks, and research (Aramburuzabala et al., 2019). Other countries still lag behind in institutionalizing Service-Learning in higher education and beyond. In this chapter, we focused on these research questions: How do teachers in higher education assess inputs, processes, and outputs of Service-Learning?

- In which ways do teachers in higher education feel institutional support for Service-Learning? (input dimension).
- Which strategies do teachers apply to approach stakeholders or community partners in order to provide Service-Learning courses? (process dimension).
- Which benefits do they associate with Service-Learning? (output dimension).

We apply a cross-country perspective, comparing the perspectives of $n = 41$ higher education teachers in Austria, Lithuania, Italy, Ireland, Portugal, and Romania on the basis of qualitative interviews about the perceived inputs, processes, and outputs of their Service-Learning courses.

INPUTS, PROCESSES, AND OUTPUTS OF SERVICE-LEARNING

Teaching in higher education is a responsibility with many facets and teachers have to balance institutional rules with personal interests and basic regulations of curricula. However, teachers play a central role in Service-Learning when they decide to offer this kind of applied coursework. Through incorporating Service-Learning projects within their teaching and research, teachers enrich their courses with multiple benefits for all involved stakeholders: students, faculty, community partners and finally also for their own professional development (Aguiniga & Bowers, 2019). An example for Service-Learning could be an economy class, in which students deliver a service to an association for the disabled, offering to support the association with their yearly cash accounting.

Students hereby learn to apply skills in accounting in a real case scenario and develop a sense of social responsibility, while delivering a service for a non-for-profit organization, which has an impact on the community. These processes, however, have to be guided and reflected with the teacher in class and embedded within the curriculum so that students learn on various levels (cognitive, emotional, and social learning).

From the institutional point of view there may be many reasons to support teachers to implement Service-Learning courses (*input dimension*): According to Eyler, Giles, Stenson, and Gray, (2001), faculty using the Service-Learning approach report improvement of student academic outcomes as well as teaching quality. Moreover, Service-Learning improves students' satisfaction with faculty, increases student retention, and improves community relations (Eyler et al., 2001). Teachers, however, are not solely responsible for implementing Service-Learning—institutional conditions have to reflect a friendly environment for applied coursework. Curricula can also contain opportunities for meaningful service experiences: Faculties should be involved in the defining of learning objectives and the role that service experiences might play in achieving these objectives in the overall curriculum. Faculties will need to make readjustments to their "syllabi, statements of course learning goals and objectives, assignments, project descriptions, reflection prompts, and feedback" in order to combine service and learning (Clayton, Bringle, & Hatcher, 2013). Also, according to Brownell and Swaner (2009), "the duration of the experience should be long enough to be meaningful". Hence, there should be enough time to build relationships between teachers, students, and community partners and this should be mirrored in course structures, which should go beyond one semester. La Lopa (2012) suggests that faculties need "to determine the amount of time the students will spend on and off campus to complete the project, if and when the community partner will visit the classroom, and how, when, where, and why the faculty member will become personally involved in the learning". This involves an opening of higher education institutions to the outside and allowing community partners in their classrooms and learning processes. Also, offering a Service-Learning course is a question of access to relevant pedagogical resources and tools. Finally, also the conditions under which teachers work, influence their ability to stay up to date in didactic methods and offer Service-Learning courses. Oftentimes they work with a subcontract only, have a relatively low professional status, and have to manage crowded classrooms and a poor university infrastructure.

In terms of Service-Learning as an innovative pedagogy,[1] teachers in higher education are challenged to design and implement Service-Learning with students and community partners (*process dimension*) against the background of available institutional support. Teachers, who may be new to higher education, must make fundamental decisions before starting to offer Service-Learning courses. They must be willing to actively involve students in their coursework (Furco, 2003), to create more authentic learning situations for students, and to collaborate with community partners. Teachers must be able to identify a relevant problem that is both socially and personally significant for students and community partners (Reinders, 2016). Also, teaching a Service-Learning course requires teachers to change their role from a traditional-instructive role to a more non-hierarchical one (Howard, 2003). A recent study found that roles in Service-Learning can be divided in expert roles (teaching and instruction) and supporting roles (process managing, mediating, and guidance counselling) (Resch & Schrittesser, 2021). The continuous guidance of students' individual learning processes and the support of self-organised learning with community partners are more in the focus than in traditional teaching approaches (Zinger, 2020). Teachers' tasks in Service-Learning courses are extended, as they have to give sufficient and multiple opportunities for students' reflections. Although there is a high personal autonomy and responsibility of students in this approach, teachers also act as role models in the communication and cooperation with community partners. Unfortunately, even when reference is made to Service-Learning in universities' strategic documents, there might be limited trainings or concrete action plans for higher education teachers who support with the process of implementation.

Service-Learning pedagogies may vary based on the local context, the discipline, and the objectives and constraints of those involved (Felten & Clayton, 2011). The challenge for the teacher is to design coursework, which contributes to delivering outcomes on various levels: academic learning, civic learning, and personal growth at the same time (Felten & Clayton, 2011). Academic learning refers to a deeper understanding of

---

[1] We have no space in this chapter to elaborate on the differences between Service-Learning, internships, volunteering, community-based research etc., we recommend the following reading: Dima, Resch, Knapp, and Ciarini (2020).

theories, models, academic concepts, and research findings in a course. This might be linked to deeper knowledge of accounting or applying a specific cash flow model in our example above. Civic learning refers to gaining experience in social responsibility, e.g. in non-for-profit organizations, which enables students to connect to an association for the disabled or other community partners. Personal growth refers to developing personal values and attitudes towards diverse population groups in the community (Bringle, Ruiz, Brown, & Neeb, 2016). In the process of designing such coursework, teachers have to decide how to measure these outcomes and which types of services students should deliver: direct services (students interact with clients or residents of a community or organization and have personal contact with the community partner), indirect services (students interact behind the scenes intending to support, improve, extend or coordinate resources but with less personal contact with the community partner), research Service-Learning (students perform community-based research on a topic which is relevant for the community), or advocacy Service-Learning (students interact with policy makers or decision makers to advocate community needs) (Bringle et al., 2016). Teachers may delegate different degrees and levels of responsibility to students and offer different degrees and levels of support and guidance in the process of this coursework.

Teachers in higher education might not feel well equipped to teach applied coursework involving multiple stakeholders while at the same time enhancing academic and civic learning. Since research on Service-Learning from the teacher's perspective in higher education is rare, we can observe similarities to teacher educators, who teach applied coursework for pre-service teachers (Coffey & Lavery, 2015; Mitton-Kükner, Nelson, & Desrochers, 2010; Resch & Schrittesser, 2021). Anderson (1998) mentions that teacher educators involved in pre-service teacher education pointed out as main reasons for integrating Service-Learning into their courses the need to help new teachers to use Service-Learning as a teaching method developing the ability to reflect critically on current educational practices, a positive attitude and needed abilities as well as "to help socialize teachers in the essential moral and civic obligations of teaching".

Teachers have multiple benefits when they implement Service-Learning in their disciplines (*output dimension*). Rutti et al. (2016) summarize the literature of benefits associated with Service-Learning: Through Service-Learning projects, teachers have an opportunity to conduct action research in the community, which in turn can facilitate their understanding of teaching and learning and enhancements in classroom practices (Rutti et al., 2016). Cooperative learning with the community has been found to increase teachers' instructional productivity and motivation. They often find linkages to the community partner, which form the basis of teaching cases or good practices, journal articles, and research ideas. Service-Learning provides a connection with real world situations, facilitating understanding of theoretical concepts through creative and effective methods of teaching. This is reinforced in a study by Calvert, Kurji, and Kurji (2011), which found that Service-Learning bridges theoretical concepts with experiential learning through projects within the larger community.

It is, finally, also important to apply a critical approach to Service-Learning as a teaching approach. It is criticized for serving the objectives of higher education (faculty and staff), such as providing research laboratories for faculty members and venues for students to implement applied coursework (Holland, 2005). Instead of helping to bring about transformational change in communities, Service-Learning can become a technical practice with a "charity" orientation and in this sense mirrors a neoliberal approach in the transformation of higher education (Raddon & Harrison, 2015). Service-Learning can also be instrumentalized to appeal to external funders and attract public attention (Slaughter & Rhoades, 2000). In terms of inequality, Service-Learning might be a luxury "many students cannot afford, be it in terms of time, finances, or job future" (Butin, 2010). In order to prevent Service-Learning from becoming just one more academic practice, students should be equipped to analyze policy and society (Wohnig, 2016).

EMPIRICAL STUDY

Objectives: In the context of the European 'ENGAGE STUDENTS' project (2018–2021), we investigated the perspectives of higher education teachers in public universities on Service-Learning—perceived inputs, processes, and outputs—since there is extensive research about students' perspectives, but those of teachers are described as "relatively invisible in the discourse of service learning" (Boland, 2014). The study focused on the main research question: How do teachers in higher education assess inputs, processes, and outputs of Service-Learning?

Methodology: For the purpose of answering these questions, we conducted semi-structured interviews (King, Horrocks, & Brooks, 2019). The interview guide consisted of eight open-ended questions, asking teachers to express their opinions and experiences about available support for Service-Learning (*input dimension*), the process of preparing Service-Learning and approaching community partners (*process dimension*[2]), and about potential benefits of applying this approach (*output dimension*).

Study participants: We applied a convenience sampling strategy using the guidelines proposed by Schreier (2018), asking teachers who apply the Service-Learning approach in their teaching to participate in the interview study. In total, $n = 41$ higher education teachers participated in the study between April 4 and July 23, 2019, using a semi-structured interview guide. The participating teachers came from a range of disciplines (Marketing, Political Science, Anthropology, Pedagogy, Sociology, Computer Programming, Thermodynamics, Nutritional Sciences, Dental Medicine, Design etc.). 31 of the study participants were female, and ten were male. Five teachers came from Ireland, Lithuania, and Italy each, twelve from Austria, six from Romania, and eight from Portugal. All of the $n = 41$ interviews were conducted face-to-face and were audiotaped. The interviews were transcribed afterwards. For the purpose of this chapter and in order to adhere to standards of cross-language research (Resch & Enzenhofer, 2018), the authors asked project partners to translate the transcripts into English. All study participants gave their written consent.

Data analysis: Data analysis was carried out using structured content analysis (Mayring, 2000), starting with initial coding of interview sections, and structuring these codes along wider categories of input, process, and outputs of service learning. The sub-categories within the three main codes (input, process, and output) were developed in focused coding used to conduct a thorough comparison of the teachers' perspectives. All interviews were numbered according to country abbreviation (AT, IE, IT, LT, PT, RO) and sequential interview number (RO25, IT37 etc.).

---

[2] In the *process dimension* the research could have also focused on other aspects, however, we identified the process of approaching community partners as one of the most important tasks for the teacher, which cannot be delegated to students.

Findings

Our key findings of the interviews are structured along the input, process, and output dimension.

Input: Institutional Support for Service-Learning

Teachers in the sample reported either (1) non-supportive institutional conditions for Service-Learning or, (2) supportive institutional conditions for Service-Learning in terms of matching platforms and portals, support with contractual issues, continuous training for students, practical support, and national supportive framework conditions for Service-Learning.

Those teachers, who reported not being supported institutionally (PT30, PT33, AT16, AT22, IT37, IT39, LT10), reported no need for support or no available support at faculty level. They located reasons for not being supported in Service-Learning as not being a faculty priority (PT30, IT39) or not being in need of support (AT16). Strategies to connect Service-Learning courses do not exist in many faculties, which leads teachers to experience teaching Service-Learning "as an isolated initiative" (PT30, LT10, IE3). A teacher from Italy even reports: "*My institution does not promote service learning very much and it does not encourage and support it with adequate resources (...), so that often students have to support out of their own pocket (...) which can necessarily only be of very short duration*" (IT37). A teacher from Ireland reports that "*a lot of support is happening in silent ways*" (IE3), when people are engaged and passionate about the service they implement, however, a support framework or an overall concerted strategy is missing in many cases.

Those teachers in the sample who recognize and observe active support by their institutions, mention matching platforms and portals as supportive technology for Service-Learning (RO25, IT38). In the Romanian case, the institution uses a Moodle platform to connect students with teachers, but the platform is also used for guidance counselling and feedback. In the Italian case, there is a portal which matches community partners with the university. This leads to a transparent and traceable process of organizing placements for students. Also, support with contractual issues is mentioned (RO 4, IT38). Service-Learning projects sometimes require contractual agreements or written agreements with the community partner. Teachers herein experience support with the formal bureaucratic procedures in order to save staff resources. "*The university facilitates this by making educational contracts with high schools and technological schools*" (IT38). Practical support is observed only by one teacher: In this case, the institution offers centralized transportation for students who implement a service at the local municipality in Portugal (PT29). Transportation is organized by the faculty and is additionally supported by the purchase of food and the printing of material. Teachers also mention continuous training as a necessity in the topic of Service-Learning, which is available to them in the form of trainings, conferences, workshops, or national networks (RO27, IT37, IE1, IE3). In the rare case, that a matching office, transfer office or Office of Student Support and Development is available, teachers feel additionally supported by administrative staff (IT41, IE3). An Italian teacher (IT41) explains that three staff members were hired for finding Service-Learning placements and for matching community partners and students at their faculty. They also monitor the entire process and make a final assessment together with the teacher. Regular meetings are held with the supervisors of students, so that they can monitor the progress and be available to their needs. In Ireland, there is also "dedicated staff" who support students in terms of guidance (IE3). The last category identified in the data for institutional support are national supportive framework conditions for Service-Learning, which is the particular case in Ireland (IE1, IE3). "*Our institution has a very strong Service-Learning ethos*" (IE1). A national network is dedicated to supporting Irish higher education institutions to promote civic and community engagement, and guidance for engaged research—for academics (working with civil society organisations), and Service-Learning—for students.

Process: Approaching Stakeholders for Service-Learning

We were particularly interested in the processes, how teachers approach and maintain stakeholder cooperation for Service-Learning. Teachers reported maintaining existing relationships with stakeholders in continuous communication processes on the one hand and on the other hand approaching new stakeholders through a variety of methodologies. We identified two main categories in the data: Teachers differentiated between (1) self-signaling stakeholders, who approach the higher education institution on their own initiative, and (2) promotion strategies for approaching stakeholders on behalf of the higher education institution.

First, teachers from all countries represented in the sample reported self-signaling stakeholders or community partners (PT32, AT15, AT19, LT10, IE5), which shows that teachers maintain existing relationships with stakeholders and thus provide regular opportunities for mutual Service-Learning projects. A teacher from Austria who implements Service-Learning in schools, states that once schools know about the possibility to cooperate with the university, they *"register regularly"* (AT15). The advantages of self-signaling stakeholders are less coordinated action on behalf of the university, better established relationships and mutual trust, and better understanding of needs (AT19). A teacher from Lithuania explains that the incentive to participate in Service-Learning activities stems from companies in their case. *"Companies provide specific tasks for a particular module taught at university and ask for solving a significant problem in their business context. The question comes from the business partner and students are asked to help solve the issue at hand"* (LT10).

Second, a number of promotion strategies are used in order to attract stakeholders or community partners to Service-Learning projects, e.g. formal or informal meetings with communities, municipalities, non-for-profit organizations, business partners etc. (PT29, PT30), presentations (PT29), written material (PT29, RO27), or (social) media promotion (RO24, RO27). Networks are also useful to disseminate Service-Learning initiatives (e.g. student unions, student associations, career counselling centers, business networks, charities etc.). A teacher from Romania who frequently implements social media strategies via Facebook, Linkedin and Twitter, however, states: *"Still, the direct approach for participation was the best result strategy"* (RO24). Thus, the most successful promotion strategy to approach stakeholders is through teachers' or students' direct contact to community partners. They stress the relevance of a personal trust relationship, interpersonal communication, active communication, and the continuity of work (LT7, LT8). Finding and working on a common objective was viewed as an advantage of a direct collaboration, which leads to benefits on all sides. The teachers in the sample report direct strategies to approach partners and reflect upon the effort of continuous communication, which was described as open, trustworthy, and directed towards mutual benefits (AT18, LT7). *"I presented the service learning (project), outlining the aims, the type of collaboration that was desired, the advantages that would derive from joining this experience"* (IT40). Either professors or teachers contact partners (PT31, RO23, IE5) or students have ideas for placements when they work in companies or in the community (PT31, PT32). Teachers explain their role as a match-maker role, communicating actively, and taking the initiative (IE2). "*I maintain the permanent communication with schools and high schools*" (RO26). We conclude that maintaining stakeholder contact is a characteristic of good quality Service-Learning, and not a one-time experience for a community partner.

Outputs: Benefits from Service-Learning

Service-Learning was mentioned to bear specific outputs for students, universities, and the communities involved. Most benefits were viewed on the side of the students.

On the *student level*, teachers perceive an impact for students in skills development, contribution to civic engagement, acquisition of work-related skills, and outputs for personal growth and development.

Teachers view Service-Learning as coursework, which is applied and leads to closing the gap between theory and practice (PT29, PT30, RO28, LT6, AT13 AT14, AT21). Students acquire skills, which derive from their intensive connection to practical fields of work and which could not arise from theory classes. Applied coursework enables them to apply problem-solving skills or theory from class in practice and to touch upon real-life problems (LT6, IE1).

In terms of skills acquisition, teachers from all countries mention the following as important outputs on student level (RO25, RO27, RO29, IE2, AT13, AT17, PT31, IT38, LT8): innovation skills, problem solving skills, project management skills, transferable skills, teamwork, leadership skills, empathy, entrepreneurial skills, acquire the ability to work in groups (teamworking), leadership, to take on responsibilities, to respect delivery times and deadlines, to take the initiative, to rationalize work, to reflect upon an adequate "working personality" etc. "*Students typically don't get executive and managerial experience, and service learning gives direct contact with managerial staff, opportunities to relate their learning experience to what they have been taught and see how useful and realistic it is*" (IE1). Students learn to develop pro-active solutions and be active in a problem-solving process (RO27). One teacher describes that "*students not only gained the ability to solve real community's problems, but also improved their empathy, for example understanding of the motivations and needs of community members, moral provisions and a sense of solidarity.*

(...) The students' involvement in these activities leads to improved social skills, such as an ability to work in a team and to interact with different people, and also communication skills and the ability to behave in a given situation. (...) The ability to perceive community members' otherness leads to effective communication and collaboration and the ability to create inter-personal relationships" (LT8). Other teachers in the sample also mention an increase in social capital of students as an output of Service-Learning and that students are likely to maintain contacts with people from the community after the service activity has ended (AT11, AT14, AT19, AT21).

Service-Learning also contributes to the development of social responsibility and civic engagement in students (IT37, LT8). Teachers in the sample recognize that applied coursework also has a social dimension apart from contents and technical considerations and start thinking about real-life implications of their work (PT32), such as community needs, problems of corruption, territorial problems etc. *"During the Service-Learning process, students turn from passive 'recipients' of information into active learners, who study all the time, monitor changes in their knowledge, skills and regulations"* (LT8).

Teachers emphasize the development of work-related skills and positive implications of Service-Learning for professional life (PT37, AT21, RO24, RO27, IE2). Teachers mention advantages for students' CVs, portfolios, and early career. Students gain understandings for an actual work environment and develop professional skills (IE2). In terms of personal development, teachers emphasize that students expand their horizon, develop empathy for diverse needs, and reflect their own values and behaviour (RO27, LT7).

Service-Learning is assessed as a form of applied coursework, which can also achieve long-term, not intentional outputs, e.g. when students continue to maintain a relationship after service learning has ended or continue to meet other students (IT40). Also, some students found their own initiatives or informal groups after their Service-Learning experience (IT40, IE1).

From an *institutional perspective*, Service-Learning contributes to reducing the stereotyping of universities as too theoretical or 'unreachable' for real needs and allowing them to be perceived as socially responsible institutions that are embedded in their communities (AT10, AT12, AT16, AT17). *"I think it [Service-Learning] is an important step in bringing the university closer to society and perhaps even escaping a little from the stereotype – what does sitting in an ivory tower at a university have to do with real life?"* (AT12).

Teachers in the sample also strongly believe that institutional requirements are changing and that universities are increasingly being asked to bridge the gap between theory and practice (AT21, AT17). *"The university profits through the gearing between university and practice, which is integral part of service learning, in which both parts move closer to one another"* (AT17). Teachers improve their pedagogical competences (LT8) and remain attentive to bridging the gap between theory and practice (IE5). *"It also helps teachers remain refreshed by bridging theoretical framework in academic practice with community practice"* (IE5). They also mention the permanent exchange of knowledge, skills, ideas, and synergies (PT29). Also, teachers gain social capital as service learning *"expands their circle of contacts and communication channels"* (LT7).

Teachers report specific *outputs for community partners* as well, in particular related to the respective topic of the Service-Learning project (e.g. new ideas for community waste management, innovative bicycle trails for the tourism sector, strategies to influence eating habits of lonely, older people, etc.), depending on the discipline in which Service-Learning is performed (PT29, PT30, AT22). Community partners advance their skills and engage in a constant dialogue and mutual learning opportunities with students until the output is achieved. They benefit from (advanced) students' skilled labour force (RO24). Receiving feedback was also mentioned (AT22, PT32, LT7) and contributing to community development, e.g. inclusion of migrants into the community (IT37, LT7). *"The project generated outputs not only on the cultural level (events, exhibitions, walks, street art, etc.), but on the level of the image of the neighborhood and consequently helped to redefine the sense of local identity and civic engagement. It favours dialogue with migrant communities, helping to reduce the sense of isolation, misunderstandings and stigma that characterizes migrant communities"* (IT37).

Critical Appraisal

There were nonetheless some ambivalent views on the appropriateness of Service-Learning in the higher education context. Teachers reflect critically on the overlaps between Service-Learning and volunteering and on whether or not students should be 'forced' into Service-Learning in a study programme. Moreover, those who had previously worked with vulnerable population groups and/or the disabled are more critical about students taking over what should be a paid service and see an element of risk for workforce exploitation in this approach. One reason for this could be their knowledge of the high demands that working with such diverse groups entails (AT11, AT13, AT21). Furthermore, Service-Learning is at risk of benefiting only certain students from a Western, white, and hegemonial perspective, if the service is implemented by privileged individuals, who try helping others, for example, an indigenous community (IE2). A positive effect can be raising awareness for diverse needs in students, among privileged highly educated young people, but teachers fear that this does not have a lasting effect.

CONCLUSION AND DISCUSSION

The evidence base for Service-Learning in higher education has grown worldwide in the last years, however, it remains open how to measure the various outcomes of Service-Learning coursework on both student and teacher level. This study contributes to gaining insight into the teacher's perspective as well as the input and the process dimension, which are rather under-researched to date, while the output dimension has received attention already (e.g. Rutti et al., 2016).

While the interviewed teachers assess the outputs of Service-Learning as manifold, institutional support (*input dimension*) is either not available, not needed, or depends on the institutional ethos for Service-Learning. We argue that in the future we need to strengthen the input dimension and faculties' roles in matching courses and community needs. The "silent support" perceived by teachers in our study has to be turned into visible and traceable support strategies available to all teachers on faculty level. From the institutional point of view there may be many reasons to support teachers in the process of implementing Service-Learning courses, however, real support strategies are still rare on a faculty level. Nevertheless, many faculties are slowly improving their support strategies when it comes to managing community partners with the help of online platforms and portals or transfer offices. This supports the process of approaching and maintaining contact with community partners (*process dimension*). This study shows that although Service-Learning is perceived as a method of applied coursework with various benefits for students, institutions, and the community (*output dimension*), inputs and outputs are generally out of balance according to the interview data.

Maintaining stakeholder contact is one of the main characteristics of good quality Service-Learning as approaching community partners takes time. Service-Learning should not be a one-time experience for a community partner; hence, teachers need time to keep in touch and build trust relationships. Keeping these contacts and continuously approaching them is a timely effort for teachers, which is not fully rewarded or recognized by higher education institutions to date. As a result, the question of the actual visibility of Service-Learning activities in higher education institutions for communities remains unsolved. An exception are those countries, in which national networks for Service-Learning exist (e.g. Ireland in our sample), but also Spain or Germany (Aramburuzabala et al., 2019). These national networks help to increase the visibility of cooperation opportunities between higher education institutions and communities. Permanent maintenance of cooperation needs resources teachers and researchers do not have in most cases and are not part of their contracts or responsibilities—thus the voluntary character of Service-Learning is reinforced and the missing formal and informal recognition of Service-Learning are detrimental for the further establishment of (national or local) networks.

The interviews took place in different higher education systems in Austria, Lithuania, Italy, Ireland, Portugal, and Romania—countries, which have different national policies, implementation levels of educational reforms, and infiltration of new didactic approaches. This may affect the inputs and processes of Service-Learning for higher education teachers and, consequently, for community partners. Also, the countries participating in the study might host different forms of relationship between 'organizations of practice' and higher education institutions, which might not in all cases be self-evident and smooth or supported by higher education policy. This is displayed in the fact that some interviewees speak of national networks for Service-Learning in their countries, which affect the available inputs for them, while others do not have such resources.

Finally, our study found positive effects of the availability of online portals and platforms used in Service-Learning for multiple purposes (feedback tools, matching tools, etc.). According to the interviewed teachers, the role of supportive technology for Service-Learning ('e-Service-Learning') should be considered more in the future of Service-Learning, in which students are enrolled in distance learning courses (Laurie, 2020). Currently, higher education institutions are desperately in need of developing digital solutions for Service-Learning and are working to provide e-Service-Learning due to enhanced digitalization and growing risks of pandemics, while at the same time having to provide placements in practice for students. According to a recent study, e-Service-Learning holds massive potential to transform both Service-Learning and online learning by freeing Service-Learning from geographical constraints (Waldner, McGorry, & Widener, 2012)—a topic which will need to be further explored in the future.

REFERENCES

Aguiniga, D. M., & Bowers, P. H. (2019). Transforming our teaching, incorporating service learning into macro practice social work classes. *The Journal of Service Learning in Higher Education, 9*, 1–7. https://journals.sfu.ca/jslhe/index.php/jslhe/article/view/179. Accessed 15 October 2020.

Anderson, J. (1998). *Service learning and teacher education.* ERIC Clearinghouse on Teaching and Teacher Education Washington DC. http://ericae.net/edo/ed421481.htm. Accessed 15 October 2020.

Aramburuzabala, P., McIlrath, L., & Opazo, H. (Eds.). (2019). *Embedding service learning in European higher education: Developing a culture of civic engagement.* London: Routledge.

Boland, J. A. (2014). Orientations to civic engagement: Insights into the sustainability of a challenging pedagogy. *Studies in Higher Education, 39*(1), 180–195.

Bringle, R. G., Ruiz, A. I., Brown, A. I., & Neeb, R. N. (2016). Enhancing the psychology curriculum through service learning. *Psychology Learning & Technology, 15*(3), 294–309.

Bringle, R. G., Hatcher, J., & McIntosh, R. (2006). Analyzing Morton's typology of service paradigms and integrity. *Michigan Journal of Community Service Learning, 13*(1), 5–15.

Brownell, J. E., & Swaner, L. E. (2009). High-impact practices: Applying the learning outcomes literature to the development of successful campus programs. *Peer Review, 11*(2), 26–30.

Butin, D. W. (2010). *Service-learning in theory and practice: The future of community engagement in higher education.* New York: Palgrave Macmillan.

Calvert, V., Kurji, R., & Kurji, S. (2011). Service learning for accounting students: What is the faculty role? *Research in Higher Education Journal, 10*, 1–11.

Campus Compact. (1985). *Campus Compact overview.* https://compact.org/who-we-are/. Accessed 15 October 2020.

Campus Outreach Opportunity League. (1984). https://orgs.tigweb.org/campus-outreach-opportunity-league. Accessed 15 October 2020.

Clayton, P. H., Bringle, R. G., & Hatcher, J. A. (Eds.). (2013). *Research on service learning: Conceptual frameworks and assessment. Volume 2A: Students and faculty.* Sterling, VA: Stylus Publishing.

Coffey, A., & Lavery, S. (2015). Service-learning: A valuable means of preparing pre-service teachers for a teaching practicum. *Australian Journal of Teacher Education, 40*(7), 1–17.

Darling-Hammond, L. (2017). Teacher education around the world: What can we learn from international practice? *European Journal of Teacher Education, 40*(3), 291–309.

Dima, G., Resch, K., Knapp, M., & Ciarini, A. (2020). *Service learning methodology toolkit: Comparing practical teaching methods in higher education.* Project "ENGAGE STUDENTS". https://www.engagestudents.eu/wp-content/uploads/2020/10/ES-Service-Learning-Methodology-Toolkit.pdf. Accessed 15 October 2020.

Eyler, J., Giles, D. E., Stenson, C. M., & Gray, C. (2001). At a glance: What we know about the effects of service-learning on college students, faculty, institutions and communities, 1993–2000: Third edition. *Higher Education.* 139. http://digitalcommons.unomaha.edu/slcehighered/139. Accessed 15 October 2020.

Felten, P., & Clayton, P. H. (2011). Service-learning. *New Directions for Teaching and Learning, 128,* 75–84.

Furco, A. (2003). Issues of definition and program diversity in the study of service-learning. In S. Billig & A. S. Waterman (Eds.), *Studying service learning: Innovations in education research methodology* (pp. 13–33). London: Routledge.

Furco, A. (2009). Die Rolle von Service Learning im Aufbau einer gesellschaftlich engagierten Universität. In K. Altenschmidt, J. Miller, & W. Stark (Eds.), *Raus aus dem Elfenbeinturm? Entwicklungen in Service Learning und bürgerschaftlichem Engagement an deutschen Hochschulen* (pp. 47–59). Weinheim & Basel: Beltz Verlag.

Holland, B. (2005). Reflections on community-campus partnerships: What has been learned? What are the next challenges? In P. Pasque, B. Mallory, R. Smerek, B. Dwyer, & N. Bowman (Eds.), *Higher education collaboratives for community engagement and improvement* (pp. 10–17). Ann Arbor: National Forum on Higher Education for the Public Good.

Howard, J. (2003). Service-learning research: Foundational issues. In S. Billig & A. S. Waterman (Eds.), *Studying service-learning: Innovations in education research methodology account* (pp. 1–12). London: Routledge.

King, N., Horrocks, Ch., & Brooks, J. (2019). *Interviews in qualitative research.* Los Angeles, CA: Sage.

La Lopa, J. (2012). Service-learning: Connecting the classroom to the community to generate a robust and meaningful learning experience for students, faculty, and community partners. *Journal of Culinary Science & Technology, 10*(2), 168–183.

Laurie, M. M. (2020). eService-learning: Bridging online graduate students' sense of belonging with community engagement. In J. A. Delello & R. R. McWhorter (Eds.), *Disruptive and emerging technology trends across education and the workplace* (pp. 116–142). Hershey, PA: IGI Global.

Mayring, P. (2000). Qualitative content analysis. *Forum: Qualitative Research, 1*(2), Art. 20. http://www.qualitative-reserach.net/fqs-texte/2-00/02-00mayring-e.htm. Accessed 15 October 2020.

Menezes, I., Coelho, M., Amorim, J. P. (2018). Social and public responsibility, universities. In P. Teixeira & J. Shin (Eds.), *Encyclopedia of international higher education systems and institutions* (pp. 1–7). Dordrecht: Springer. https://doi.org/10.1007/978-94-017-9553-1_361-1. Accessed 15 October 2020.

Mitton-Kükner, J., Nelson, C., & Desrochers, C. (2010). Narrative inquiry in service learning contexts: Possibilities for learning about diversity in teacher education. *Teaching and Teacher Education, 26*(5), 1162–1169.

Raddon, M.-B., & Harrison, B. (2015). Is service-learning the kind face of the neo-liberal university? *Canadian Journal of Higher Education, 45*(2), 134–153.

Reinders, H. (2016). *Service Learning—Theoretische Überlegungen und empirische Studien zu Lernen durch Engagement.* Weinheim & Basel: Beltz Juventa.

Resch, K., & Enzenhofer, E. (2018). Collecting data in other languages—Strategies for cross-language research in multilingual societies. In U. Flick (Ed.), *The SAGE handbook of qualitative data collection* (pp. 131–147). London: Sage.

Resch, K., & Schrittesser, I. (2021). Using the service learning approach to bridge the gap between theory and practice in teacher education in Austria. *International Journal of Inclusive Education.* https://doi.org/10.1080/13603116.2021.1882053.

Rutti, R., LaBonte, J., Helms, M., Hervani, A., & Sarkarat, S. (2016). The service learning projects: Stakeholder benefits and potential class topics. *Education & Training, 58*(4), 422–438.

Schreier, M. (2018). Sampling and generalization. In U. Flick (Ed.), *The SAGE handbook of qualitative data collection* (pp. 84–98). London: Sage.

Slaughter, S., & Rhoades, G. (2000, Spring/Summer). The neo-liberal university. *New Labor Forum, 6,* 73–79.

Tatebe, J. (2013). Bridging gaps: Service learning in teacher education. *Pastoral Care in Education, 31*(3), 240–250.

Waldner, L. S., McGorry, S. Y., & Widener, M. C. (2012). E-Service-learning: The evolution of service-learning to engage a growing online student population. *Journal of Higher Education Outreach and Engagement, 16*(2), 123–150.

Waldstein, F. A., & Reiher, T. (2001). Service-learning and students' personal and civic. *Journal of Experiential Education, 24*(1), 7–14.

Wohnig, A. (2016). Political learning by social engagement? Chances and risks for citizenship education. *Citizenship, Social and Economics Education, 15*(3), 244–261.

Zinger, B. (2020). Die Bedeutung von Service Learning für die Hochschuldidaktik. In D. Rosenkranz, S. Roderus, & N. Obereck (Eds.), *Service Learning an Hochschulen. Konzeptionelle Überlegungen und innovative Beispiele* (pp. 116–121). Weinheim & Basel: Beltz Juventa.

INDEX